BAHÁ'Í PRAYERS

A Selection of the Prayers
Revealed by
Bahá'u'lláh, The Báb, and 'Abdu'l-Bahá

> "Blessed is the spot, and the
> house, and the place, and the
> city, and the heart, and the
> mountain, and the refuge,
> and the cave, and the valley,
> and the land, and the sea, and
> the island, and the meadow
> where mention of God hath
> been made, and His praise
> glorified."   —Bahá'u'lláh

BAHÁ'Í PUBLISHING TRUST
WILMETTE, ILLINOIS
1979

PRINTED IN THE UNITED STATES OF AMERICA

BAHÁ'Í PRAYERS
FOR GENERAL USE

"INTONE, O My servant, the verses of God that have been received by thee, as intoned by them who have drawn nigh unto Him, that the sweetness of thy melody may kindle thine own soul, and attract the hearts of all men. Whoso reciteth, in the privacy of his chamber, the verses revealed by God, the scattering angels of the Almighty shall scatter abroad the fragrance of the words uttered by his mouth, and shall cause the heart of every righteous man to throb. Though he may, at first, remain unaware of its effect, yet the virtue of the grace vouchsafed unto him must needs sooner or later exercise its influence upon his soul. Thus have the mysteries of the Revelation of God been decreed by virtue of the will of Him Who is the Source of power and wisdom."

—Bahá'u'lláh

TABLE OF CONTENTS

The headings designated are purely arbitrary, for the purpose of easier location of the prayers, and are not a part of the authentic text.

The first lines of prayers revealed by *Bahá'u'lláh* are given in italics in this Contents, as are also those for the two revealed by the Báb which are indicated as by Him. The prayers not so identified are revealed by 'Abdu'l-Bahá.

TABLE OF CONTENTS

7

TABLE OF CONTENTS

TABLE OF CONTENTS

9

Assistance

1.

My God, my Adored One, my King, my Desire! What tongue can voice my thanks to Thee? I was heedless, Thou didst awaken me. I had turned back from Thee, Thou didst graciously aid me to turn toward Thee. I was as one dead, Thou didst quicken me with the water of life. I was withered, Thou didst revive me with the heavenly stream of Thine utterance which hath flowed forth from the Pen of the All-Merciful.

O Divine Providence! All existence is begotten by Thy bounty; deprive it not of the waters of Thy generosity, neither do Thou withhold it from the ocean of Thy mercy. I beseech Thee to aid and assist me at all times and under all conditions, and seek from the heaven of Thy grace Thine ancient favor. Thou art, in truth, the Lord of bounty, and the Sovereign of the kingdom of eternity.   —*Bahá'u'lláh*

2.

O THOU Whose face is the object of my adoration, Whose beauty is my sanctuary, Whose habitation is my goal, Whose praise is my hope, Whose providence is my companion, Whose love is the cause of my being, Whose mention is my solace, Whose nearness is my desire, Whose presence is my dearest wish and highest aspiration, I entreat Thee not to withhold from me the things Thou didst ordain for the chosen ones among Thy servants. Supply me, then, with the good of this world and of the next.

Thou, truly, art the King of all men. There is no God but Thee, the Ever-Forgiving, the Most Generous. —*Bahá'u'lláh*

3.

LORD! Pitiful are we, grant us Thy favor; poor, bestow upon us a share from the ocean of Thy wealth; needy, do Thou satisfy us; abased, give us Thy glory. The fowls of the air and the beasts of the field receive their meat each day from Thee and all beings partake of Thy care and loving-kindness.

Deprive not this feeble one of Thy wondrous grace and vouchsafe by Thy might unto this helpless soul Thy bounty.

Give us our daily bread and grant Thine increase in the necessities of life; that we may be dependent on none other but Thee, may commune wholly with Thee, may walk in Thy ways and declare Thy mysteries. Thou art the Almighty and Loving and the Provider of all mankind. —'Abdu'l-Bahá

4.

REMOVE NOT, O Lord! the festal board that hath been spread in Thy Name and extinguish not the burning flame that hath been kindled by Thine unquenchable fire. Withhold not from flowing that Living Water of Thine that murmureth with the melody of Thy glory and Thy remembrance, and deprive not Thy servants from the fragrance of Thy sweet savors breathing forth the perfume of Thy love.

Lord! Turn the distressing cares of Thy holy ones into ease, their hardship into comfort, their abasement into glory, their sorrow into blissful joy; O Thou that holdest in Thy grasp the reins of all mankind!

Thou art verily the One, the Single, the Mighty, the All-Knowing, the All-Wise.

—*'Abdu'l-Bahá*

Children

5.

O God, guide me, protect me, illumine the lamp of my heart and make me a brilliant star. Thou art the Mighty and Powerful. —'*Abdu'l-Bahá*

6.

O Thou pure God! I am a little child; make Thou the bosom of Thy gift a dear resting-place of comfort, suffer me to grow and be nurtured with the honey and the milk of Thy love and train me under the breast of Thy knowledge; bestow Thou freedom while in a state of childhood and grant Thou excellence!

O Thou Incomparable One! Make me the confidant of the Kingdom of the Unseen! Verily, Thou art the Mighty and the Powerful!

—'*Abdu'l-Bahá*

7.

O MY LORD! O my Lord!

I am a child of tender years. Nourish me from the breast of Thy mercy, train me in the bosom of Thy love, educate me in the school of Thy guidance and develop me under the shadow of Thy bounty! Deliver me from darkness, make me a brilliant light; free me from unhappiness, make me a flower of the rose-garden; suffer me to become the servant of Thy Threshold and confer upon me the disposition and nature of the righteous ones; make me a cause of bounty to the human world and crown my head with the diadem of eternal life!

Verily, Thou art the Powerful, the Mighty, the Seer, the Hearer!   —'Abdu'l-Bahá

8.

O GOD! Educate these children. These children are the plants of Thine orchard, the flowers of Thy meadow, the roses of Thy garden. Let Thy rain fall upon them; let the Sun of Reality shine upon them with Thy love. Let Thy breeze refresh them in order that they may be trained, grow and develop and appear in the utmost beauty. Thou art the Giver! Thou art the Compassionate!   —'Abdu'l-Bahá

9.

O God! Rear this little babe in the bosom of Thy love and give it milk from the breast of Providence. Cultivate this fresh plant in the rose-garden of Thy love and nurture it by showers from the clouds of Providence. Make it a child of the Kingdom and lead it to the divine world. Thou art powerful and kind! Thou art the Giver, the Bestower, Whose blessings transcend all else!   —'Abdu'l-Bahá

Dawn

10.

O MY GOD and my Master! I am Thy servant
and the son of Thy servant. I have risen from
my couch at this dawn-tide when the Day-Star
of Thy oneness hath shone forth from the Day-
Spring of Thy will, and hath shed its radiance
upon the whole world, according to what had
been ordained in the Books of Thy Decree.

Praise be unto Thee, O my God, that we
have wakened to the splendors of the light of
Thy knowledge. Send down, then, upon us, O
my Lord, what will enable us to dispense with
any one but Thee, and will rid us of all attachment to aught except Thyself. Write down,
moreover, for me, and for such as are dear to
me, and for my kindred, man and woman alike,
the good of this world and the world to come.
Keep us safe, then, through Thine unfailing
protection, O Thou the Beloved of the entire

creation and the Desire of the whole universe, from them whom Thou hast made to be the manifestations of the evil whisperer, who whisper in men's breasts. Potent art Thou to do Thy pleasure. Thou art, verily, the Almighty, the Help in Peril, the Self-Subsisting.

Bless Thou, O Lord my God, Him Whom Thou hast set over Thy most excellent titles, and through Whom Thou hast divided between the godly and the wicked, and graciously aid us to do what Thou lovest and desirest. Bless Thou, moreover, O my God, them Who are Thy Words and Thy Letters, and them who have set their faces towards Thee, and turned unto Thy face, and hearkened to Thy Call.

Thou art, truly, the Lord and King of all men, and art potent over all things.

—Bahá'u'lláh

Day of God

MAGNIFIED be Thy Name, O my God, for that Thou hast manifested the Day which is the King of Days, the Day which Thou didst announce unto Thy chosen Ones and Thy Prophets in Thy most excellent Tablets, the Day whereon Thou didst shed the splendor of the glory of all Thy names upon all created things. Great is his blessedness whosoever hath set himself towards Thee, and entered Thy presence, and caught the accents of Thy voice.

I beseech Thee, O my Lord, by the name of Him round Whom circleth in adoration the kingdom of Thy names, that Thou wilt graciously assist them that are dear to Thee to glorify Thy word among Thy servants, and to shed abroad Thy praise amidst Thy creatures, so that the ecstasies of Thy Revelation may fill the souls of all the dwellers of Thine earth.

Since Thou hast guided them, O my Lord, unto the living waters of Thy grace, grant, by Thy bounty, that they may not be kept back from Thee; and since Thou hast summoned them to the habitation of Thy throne, drive them not out from Thy presence, through Thy loving-kindness. Send down upon them what shall wholly detach them from aught else except Thee, and make them able to soar in the atmosphere of Thy nearness, in such wise that neither the ascendancy of the oppressor nor the suggestions of them that have disbelieved in Thy most august and most mighty Self shall be capable of keeping them back from Thee. —*Bahá'u'lláh*

For the Departed

12.

GLORY be to Thee, O Lord my God! Abase not him whom Thou hast exalted through the power of Thine everlasting sovereignty, and remove not far from Thee him whom Thou hast caused to enter the tabernacle of Thine eternity. Wilt Thou cast away, O my God, him whom Thou hast overshadowed with Thy Lordship, and wilt Thou turn away from Thee, O my Desire, him to whom Thou hast been a refuge? Canst Thou degrade him whom Thou hast uplifted, or forget him whom Thou didst enable to remember Thee?

Glorified, immensely glorified art Thou! Thou art He Who from everlasting hath been the King of the entire creation and its Prime Mover, and Thou wilt to everlasting remain the Lord of all created things and their Ordainer. Glorified art Thou, O my God! If Thou ceasest to be merciful unto Thy servants, who, then, will show mercy unto them? and if Thou refusest to succor Thy loved ones, who is there that can succor them?

Glorified, immeasurably glorified art Thou! Thou art adored in Thy truth, and Thee do we all, verily, worship; and Thou art manifest in Thy justice, and to Thee do we all, verily, bear witness. Thou, art, in truth, beloved in Thy grace. No God is there but Thee, the Help in Peril, the Self-Subsisting. —*Bahá'u'lláh*

13.

O MY GOD! O Thou forgiver of sins! Bestower of gifts! Dispeller of afflictions!

Verily, I beseech Thee to forgive the sins of such as have abandoned the physical garment and have ascended to the spiritual world.

O my Lord! Purify them from trespasses, dispel their sorrows, and change their darkness into light. Cause them to enter the garden of happiness, cleanse them with the most pure water, and grant them to behold Thy splendors on the loftiest mount. —*'Abdu'l-Bahá*

14.

HE IS God, exalted is He, the Lord of loving-kindness and bounty!

Glory be unto Thee, Thou, O my God, the Lord Omnipotent. I testify to Thine omnipotence and Thy might, Thy sovereignty and Thy loving-kindness, Thy grace and Thy power, the oneness of Thy Being and the unity of Thine Essence, Thy sanctity and exaltation above the world of being and all that is therein.

O my God! Thou seest me detached from all save Thee, holding fast unto Thee and turning unto the ocean of Thy bounty, to the heaven of Thy favor, to the Day-Star of Thy grace.

Lord! I bear witness that in Thy servant Thou hast reposed Thy trust and that is the spirit wherewith Thou hast given life to the world.

I ask of Thee by the splendor of the Orb of Thy Revelation, mercifully to accept from him that which he hath achieved in Thy days. Grant then that he may be invested with the glory of

Thy good-pleasure and adorned with Thine acceptance.

O my Lord! I myself and all created things bear witness unto Thy might and I pray Thee not to turn away from Thyself this spirit that hath ascended unto Thee, unto Thy heavenly place, Thine exalted Paradise and Thy retreats of nearness.

O Thou who art the Lord of all men! Grant then, O my God, that Thy servant may consort with Thy chosen ones, Thy saints and Thy Messengers in heavenly places that the pen cannot tell nor the tongue recount.

O my Lord, the poor one hath verily hastened unto the Kingdom of Thy wealth, the stranger unto his home within Thy precincts, he that is sore athirst to the heavenly river of Thy bounty. Deprive him not, O Lord, from his share of the banquet of Thy grace and from the favor of Thy bounty. Thou art in truth the Almighty, the Gracious, the All-Bountiful!

O my God, Thy trust hath been returned unto Thee. It behooveth Thy grace and Thy bounty that have compassed Thy dominions on earth and in heaven, to vouchsafe unto Thy newly welcomed one Thy gifts and Thy bestowals, and the fruits of the tree of Thy grace!

Powerful art Thou to do as Thou willest. There is none other God but Thee, the Gracious, the Most Bountiful, the Compassionate, the Bestower, the Pardoner, the Precious, the All-Knowing.

I testify, O my Lord, that Thou hast enjoined upon men to honor their guest, and he that hath ascended unto Thee hath verily reached Thee and attained Thy Presence. Deal with him then according to Thy grace and bounty! By Thy glory, I know of a certainty that Thou wilt not deny Thyself from that which Thou hast commanded Thy servants, nor wilt Thou deprive him that hath clung to the cord of Thy bounty and hast ascended to the Day-Spring of Thy wealth.

There is none other God but Thee, the One, the Single, the Powerful, the Omniscient, the Bountiful.

—*Bahá'u'lláh*

Evening

15.

O MY God, my Master, the Goal of my desire! This, Thy servant, seeketh to sleep in the shelter of Thy mercy, and to repose beneath the canopy of Thy grace, imploring Thy care and Thy protection.

I beg of Thee, O my Lord, by Thine eye that sleepeth not, to guard mine eyes from beholding aught beside Thee. Strengthen, then, their vision that they may discern Thy signs, and behold the Horizon of Thy Revelation. Thou art He before the revelations of Whose omnipotence the quintessence of power hath trembled.

No God is there but Thee, the Almighty, the All-Subduing, the Unconditioned.

—*Bahá'u'lláh*

16.

How can I choose to sleep, O God, my God, when the eyes of them that long for Thee are wakeful because of their separation from Thee; and how can I lie down to rest whilst the souls of Thy lovers are sore vexed in their remoteness from Thy presence?

I have committed, O my Lord, my spirit and my entire being into the right hand of Thy might and Thy protection, and I lay my head on my pillow through Thy power, and lift it up according to Thy will and Thy good-pleasure. Thou art, in truth, the Preserver, the Keeper, the Almighty, the Most Powerful.

By Thy might! I ask not, whether sleeping or waking, but that which Thou dost desire. I am Thy servant and in Thy hands. Do Thou graciously aid me to do what will shed forth the fragrance of Thy good pleasure. This, truly, is my hope and the hope of them that enjoy near access to Thee. Praised be Thou, O Lord of the worlds!

—*Bahá'u'lláh*

17.

O seeker of Truth! If thou desirest that God may open thy (spiritual) eye, thou must supplicate unto God, pray to and commune with Him at midnight, saying:

O LORD, I have turned my face unto Thy Kingdom of oneness and am immersed in the sea of Thy mercy! O Lord, enlighten my sight by beholding Thy lights in this dark night, and make me happy by the wine of Thy love in this wonderful age! O Lord, make me hear Thy call, and open before my face the doors of Thy heaven, so that I may see the light of Thy glory and become attracted to Thy beauty!

Verily, Thou art the Giver, the Generous, the Merciful, the Forgiving!   *—'Abdu'l-Bahá*

Forgiveness

18.

GLORIFIED art Thou, O Lord my God! I beseech Thee by Thy chosen Ones, and by the Bearers of Thy Trust, and by Him Whom Thou hast ordained to be the Seal of Thy Prophets and of Thy Messengers, to let Thy remembrance be my companion, and Thy love my aim, and Thy face my goal, and Thy name my lamp, and Thy wish my desire, and Thy pleasure my delight.

I am a sinner, O my Lord, and Thou art the Ever-Forgiving. As soon as I recognized Thee, I hastened to attain the exalted court of Thy loving-kindness. Forgive me, O my Lord, my sins which have hindered me from walking in the ways of Thy good-pleasure, and from attaining the shores of the ocean of Thy oneness.

There is no one, O my Lord, who can deal bountifully with me to whom I can turn my face, and none who can have compassion on me that I may crave his mercy. Cast me not out, I implore Thee, of the presence of Thy grace, neither do Thou withhold from me the outpourings of Thy generosity and bounty. Ordain for me, O my Lord, what Thou hast ordained for them that love Thee, and write down for me what Thou hast written down for Thy chosen ones. My gaze hath, at all times, been fixed on the horizon of Thy gracious providence, and mine eyes bent upon the court of Thy tender mercies. Do with me as beseemeth Thee. No God is there but Thee, the God of power, the God of glory, Whose help is implored by all men.

—Bahá'u'lláh

19.

I AM HE, O my Lord, that hath set his face towards Thee, and fixed his hope on the wonders of Thy grace and the revelations of Thy bounty. I pray Thee that Thou wilt not suffer me to turn away disappointed from the door of Thy mercy, nor abandon me to such of Thy creatures as have repudiated Thy Cause.

I am, O my God, Thy servant and the son of Thy servant. I have recognized Thy truth in Thy days, and have directed my steps toward the shores of Thy oneness, confessing Thy singleness, acknowledging Thy unity, and hoping for Thy forgiveness and pardon. Powerful art Thou to do what Thou willest; no God is there beside Thee, the All-Glorious, the Ever-Forgiving.   —*Bahá'u'lláh*

20.

THOU seest me, O my Lord, with my face turned toward the heaven of Thy bounty and the ocean of Thy favor, withdrawn from all else beside Thee. I ask of Thee, by the splendors of the Sun of Thy Revelation on Sinai, and the effulgences of the Orb of Thy grace which shineth from the horizon of Thy Name, the Ever-Forgiving, to grant me Thy pardon and to have mercy upon me. Write down, then, for me with Thy pen of glory that which will exalt me through Thy Name in the world of creation. Aid me, O my Lord, to set myself toward Thee, and to hearken unto the voice of Thy loved ones, whom the powers of the earth have failed to weaken, and the dominion of the nations has been powerless to withhold from Thee, and who, advancing toward Thee, have said: "God is our Lord, the Lord of all who are in heaven and all who are on earth!"

—*Bahá'u'lláh*

21.

LAUDED BE Thy Name, O my God and the God of all things, my Glory and the Glory of all things, my Desire and the Desire of all things, my Strength and the Strength of all things, my King and the King of all things, my Possessor and the Possessor of all things, my Aim and the Aim of all things, my Mover and the Mover of all things! Suffer me not, I implore Thee, to be kept back from the ocean of Thy tender mercies, nor to be far removed from the shores of nearness to Thee.

Aught else except Thee, O my Lord, profiteth me not, and near access to any one save Thyself availeth me nothing. I entreat Thee by the plenteousness of Thy riches, whereby Thou didst dispense with all else except Thyself, to number me with such as have set their faces toward Thee, and arisen to serve Thee.

Forgive, then, O my Lord, Thy servants and Thy handmaidens. Thou, truly, art the Ever-Forgiving, the Most Compassionate.

—Bahá'u'lláh

22.

O Lord! O Thou hope of people! Thou art the shelter of all these Thy servants. Thou knowest the secrets and mysteries. We are all sinners and Thou art the shelter of sinners, the Merciful, the Clement. O Lord! look not at our shortcomings. Deal with us according to Thy grace and bestowal. Our shortcomings are many but the ocean of Thy forgiveness is boundless. Therefore confirm and strengthen us. Assist us in that which will make us acceptable at Thy threshold. Illumine the hearts, make the eyes seeing, render the ears attentive, resuscitate the dead and heal the sick. Render the poor rich and the fugitive confident. Accept us in Thy kingdom. Illumine us with the light of kindness. Thou art the Generous! Thou art the Clement! Thou art the Kind!

—'Abdu'l-Bahá

Healing

23.

O God, my God! I beg of Thee by the ocean of Thy healing, and by the splendors of the Day-Star of Thy grace, and by Thy Name through which Thou didst subdue Thy servants, and by the pervasive power of Thy most exalted Word and the potency of Thy most august Pen, and by Thy mercy that hath preceded the creation of all who are in heaven and on earth, to purge me with the waters of Thy bounty from every affliction and disorder, and from all weakness and feebleness.

Thou seest, O my Lord, Thy suppliant waiting at the door of Thy bounty, and him who hath set his hopes on Thee clinging to the cord of Thy generosity. Deny him not, I beseech Thee, the things he seeketh from the ocean of Thy grace and the Day-Star of Thy loving-kindness.

Powerful art Thou to do what pleaseth Thee. There is none other God save Thee, the Ever-Forgiving, the Most Generous. —*Bahá'u'lláh*

24.

THY NAME is my healing, O my God, and remembrance of Thee is my remedy. Nearness to Thee is my hope, and love for Thee is my companion. Thy mercy to me is my healing and my succor in both this world and the world to come. Thou, verily, art the All-Bountiful, the All-Knowing, the All-Wise. —*Bahá'u'lláh*

25.

PRAISED BE Thou, O Lord my God! I implore Thee by Thy Most Great Name through which Thou didst stir up Thy servants and build up Thy cities, and by Thy most excellent titles, and Thy most august attributes, to assist Thy people to turn in the direction of Thy manifold bounties, and set their faces toward the Tabernacle of Thy wisdom. Heal Thou the sicknesses that have assailed the souls on every side, and have deterred them from directing their gaze toward the Paradise that lieth in the shelter of Thy shadowing Name, which Thou didst ordain to be the King of all names unto all who are in heaven and all who are on earth. Potent art Thou to do as pleaseth Thee. In Thy hands is the empire of all names. There is none other God but Thee, the Mighty, the Wise.

I am but a poor creature, O my Lord; I have clung to the hem of Thy riches. I am sore sick; I have held fast the cord of Thy healing. Deliver me from the ills that have encircled me, and wash me thoroughly with the waters of Thy graciousness and mercy, and attire me with the raiment of wholesomeness, through Thy forgiveness and bounty. Fix, then, mine eyes upon Thee, and rid me of all attachment to aught else except Thyself. Aid me to do what Thou desirest, and to fulfill what Thou pleasest.

Thou art truly the Lord of this life and of the next. Thou art, in truth, the Ever-Forgiving, the Most Merciful.   —*Bahá'u'lláh*

26.

GLORY BE to Thee, O Lord my God! I implore Thee by Thy Name, through which Thou didst lift up the ensigns of Thy guidance, and didst shed the radiance of Thy loving-kindness, and didst reveal the sovereignty of Thy Lordship; through which the lamp of Thy names hath appeared within the niche of Thine attributes, and He Who is the Tabernacle of Thy unity and the Manifestation of detachment hath shone forth; through which the ways of Thy guidance were made known, and the paths of Thy good pleasure were marked out; through which the foundations of error have been made to tremble, and the signs of wickedness have been abolished; through which the fountains of wisdom have burst forth, and the heavenly table hath been sent down; through which Thou didst preserve Thy servants and didst vouchsafe Thy healing; through which Thou didst show forth Thy tender mercies unto Thy servants and revealedst Thy forgiveness amidst Thy creatures —I implore Thee to keep safe him who hath held fast and returned unto Thee, and clung to Thy mercy, and seized the hem of Thy loving providence. Send down, then, upon him Thy healing, and make him whole, and endue him with a constancy vouchsafed by Thee, and a tranquillity bestowed by Thy Highness.

Thou art, verily, the Healer, the Preserver,

the Helper, the Almighty, the Powerful, the All-Glorious, the All-Knowing.   —*Bahá'u'lláh*

27.

GLORY BE to Thee, O Lord my God! I beg of Thee by Thy Name through which He Who is Thy Beauty hath been stablished upon the throne of Thy Cause, and by Thy Name through which Thou changest all things, and gatherest together all things, and callest to account all things, and rewardest all things, and preservest all things, and sustainest all things— I beg of Thee to guard this handmaiden who hath fled for refuge to Thee, and hath sought the shelter of Him in Whom Thou Thyself art manifest, and hath put her whole trust and confidence in Thee.

She is sick, O my God, and hath entered beneath the shadow of the Tree of Thy healing; afflicted, and hath fled to the City of Thy protection; diseased, and hath sought the Fountain-Head of Thy favors; sorely vexed, and hath hasted to attain the Well-Spring of Thy tranquillity; burdened with sin, and hath set her face toward the court of Thy forgiveness.

Attire her, by Thy sovereignty and Thy loving-kindness, O my God and my Beloved, with the raiment of Thy balm and Thy healing, and make her quaff of the cup of Thy mercy and Thy favors. Protect her, moreover, from every affliction and ailment, from all pain and sickness, and from whatsoever may be abhorrent unto Thee.

Thou, in truth, art immensely exalted above all else except Thyself. Thou art, verily, the Healer, the All-Sufficing, the Preserver, the Ever-Forgiving, the Most Merciful.

—*Bahá'u'lláh*

Mankind

28.

MY GOD, Whom I worship and adore! I bear witness unto Thy unity and Thy oneness, and acknowledge Thy gifts, both in the past and in the present. Thou art the All-Bountiful, the overflowing showers of Whose mercy have rained down upon high and low alike, and the splendors of Whose grace have been shed over both the obedient and the rebellious.

O God of mercy, before Whose door the quintessence of mercy hath bowed down, and round the sanctuary of Whose Cause loving-kindness, in its inmost spirit, hath circled, we beseech Thee, entreating Thine ancient grace, and seeking Thy present favor, that Thou mayest have mercy upon all who are the manifestations of the world of being, and to deny them not the outpourings of Thy grace in Thy days.

All are but poor and needy, and Thou, verily, art the All-Possessing, the All-Subduing, the All-Powerful!   *—Bahá'u'lláh*

29.

LAUDED BE Thy Name, O Lord my God! Darkness hath fallen upon every land, and the forces of mischief have encompassed all the nations. Through them, however, I perceive the splendors of Thy wisdom, and discern the brightness of the light of Thy providence.

They that are shut out as by a veil from Thee have imagined that they have the power to put out Thy light, and to quench Thy fire, and to still the winds of Thy grace. Nay, and to this Thy might beareth me witness! Had not every tribulation been made the bearer of Thy wisdom, and every ordeal the vehicle of Thy providence, no one would have dared oppose us, though the powers of earth and heaven were to be leagued against us. Were I to unravel the wondrous mysteries of Thy wisdom which are laid bare before me, the reins of Thine enemies would be cleft asunder.

Glorified be Thou, then, O my God! I beseech Thee by Thy Most Great Name to assemble them that love Thee around the Law that streameth from the good-pleasure of Thy will, and to send down upon them what will assure their hearts.

Potent art Thou to do what pleaseth Thee. Thou art, verily, the Help in Peril, the Self-Subsisting. —*Bahá'u'lláh*

30.

O KIND LORD! Thou Who art generous and merciful! We are the servants of Thy threshold and we are under the protection of Thy mercy. The Sun of Thy providence is shining upon all and the clouds of Thy mercy shower upon all. Thy gifts encompass all, Thy providence sustains all, Thy protection overshadows all and the glances of Thy favor illumine all. O Lord! Grant unto us Thine infinite bestowals and let Thy light of guidance shine. Illumine the eyes, make joyous the souls and confer a new spirit upon the hearts. Give them eternal life. Open the doors of Thy knowledge; let the light of faith shine. Unite and bring mankind into one shelter beneath the banner of Thy protection, so that they may become as waves of one sea, as leaves and branches of one tree, and may assemble beneath the shadow of the same tent. May they drink from the same fountain. May they be refreshed by the same breezes. May

they obtain illumination from the same source
of light and life. Thou art the Giver, the Merciful!   —'Abdu'l-Bahá

31.

O Thou compassionate Lord! Thou Who art
generous and able! We are servants of Thine
sheltered beneath Thy providence. Cast Thy
glance of favor upon us. Give light to our eyes,
hearing to our ears and understanding and love
to our hearts. Render our souls joyous and
happy through Thy glad-tidings. O Lord! Point
out to us the pathway of Thy Kingdom and resuscitate all of us through the breaths of the
Holy Spirit. Bestow upon us life everlasting and
confer upon us never-ending honor. Unify mankind and illumine the world of humanity. May
we all follow Thy pathway, long for Thy good-
pleasure and seek the mysteries of Thy Kingdom. O God! Unite us and connect our hearts
with Thy indissoluble bond. Verily, Thou art
the Giver, Thou art the Kind One and Thou
art the Almighty!   —'Abdu'l-Bahá

32.

O Thou kind Lord! Thou hast created all humanity from the same original parents. Thou hast intended that all belong to the same household. In Thy Holy Presence they are Thy servants and all mankind are sheltered beneath Thy Tabernacle. All have gathered at Thy table of bounty and are radiant through the light of Thy providence. O God! Thou art kind to all, Thou hast provided for all, Thou dost shelter all, Thou dost confer life upon all. Thou hast endowed all with talents and faculties; all are submerged in the ocean of Thy mercy. O Thou kind Lord! unite all, let the religions agree, make the nations one so that they may be as one kind and as children of the same fatherland. May they associate in unity and concord. O God! upraise the standard of the oneness of humankind. O God! establish the Most Great Peace. Cement the hearts together, O God! O Thou kind Father, God! exhilarate the hearts through the fragrance of Thy love; brighten the eyes through the light of Thy guidance; cheer the hearing with the melodies of Thy Word and shelter us in the cave of Thy providence.

Thou art the Mighty and Powerful! Thou art the Forgiving and Thou art the One Who overlookest the shortcomings of humankind.

—'Abdu'l-Bahá

Meetings

33.

GLORIFIED art Thou, O Lord my God! I implore Thee by the onrushing winds of Thy grace, and by them Who are the Day-Springs of Thy purpose and the Dawning-Places of Thine inspiration, to send down upon me and upon all that have sought Thy face that which beseemeth Thy generosity and bountiful grace, and is worthy of Thy bestowals and favors. Poor and desolate I am, O my Lord! Immerse me in the ocean of Thy wealth; athirst, suffer me to drink from the living waters of Thy loving-kindness.

I beseech Thee, by Thine own Self and by Him Whom Thou hast appointed as the Manifestation of Thine own Being and Thy discriminating Word unto all that are in heaven and on earth, to gather together Thy servants beneath the shade of the Tree of Thy gracious providence. Help them, then, to partake of its fruits, to incline their ears to the rustling of its leaves, and to the sweetness of the voice of the Bird that chanteth upon its branches. Thou art, verily, the Help in Peril, the Inaccessible, the Almighty, the Most Bountiful. —*Bahá'u'lláh*

34.

O Thou merciful God! O Thou Who art mighty and powerful! O Thou most kind father! These servants have gathered together, turning to Thee, supplicating Thy threshold, desiring Thine endless bounties from Thy great assurance. They have no purpose save Thy good-pleasure. They have no intention save service to the world of humanity. O God! Make this assemblage radiant. Make the hearts merciful. Confer the bounties of the Holy Spirit. Endow them with a power from heaven. Bless them with heavenly minds. Increase their sincerity so that with all humility and contrition they may turn to Thy Kingdom and be occupied with service to the world of humanity. May each one become a radiant candle. May each one become a brilliant star. May each one become beautiful in color and redolent of fragrance in the Kingdom of God. O kind Father! Confer Thy blessings. Consider not our shortcomings. Shelter us under Thy protection. Remember not our sins. Heal us with Thy mercy. We are weak; Thou art mighty. We are poor; Thou art rich. We are sick; Thou art the Physician. We are needy; Thou art most generous. O God! Endow us with Thy providence. Thou art the Powerful! Thou art the Giver! Thou art the Beneficent!

—*'Abdu'l-Bahá*

35.

O Thou kind Lord! These are Thy servants who have gathered in this meeting, turned unto Thy Kingdom and are in need of Thy bestowal and blessing. O Thou God! Manifest and make evident the signs of Thy oneness which have been deposited in all the realities of life. Reveal and unfold the virtues which Thou hast made latent and concealed in these human realities. O God! We are as plants and Thy bounty is as the rain. Refresh and cause these plants to grow through Thy bestowal. We are Thy servants; free us from the fetters of material existence. We are ignorant; make us wise. We are dead; make us alive. We are material; endow us with spirit. We are deprived; make us the intimates

of Thy mysteries. We are needy; enrich and
bless us from Thy boundless treasury. O God!
Resuscitate us, give us sight, give us hearing.
Familiarize us with the mysteries of life, so that
the secrets of Thy Kingdom may become revealed to us in this world of existence and we
may confess Thy oneness. Every bestowal em-
anates from Thee; every benediction is Thine.
Thou art mighty! Thou art powerful! Thou art
the Giver and Thou art the Ever-Bounteous!

—*'Abdu'l-Bahá*

36.

O MY GOD! O my God! Verily these servants
are turning to Thee, supplicating Thy kingdom
of mercy. Verily they are attracted by Thy holiness and set aglow with the fire of Thy love, seeking confirmation from Thy wondrous Kingdom
and hoping for attainment in Thy heavenly
realm. Verily they long for the descent of Thy bestowal, desiring illumination from the Sun of
Reality. O Lord! make them radiant lamps, merciful signs, fruitful trees and shining stars. May
they come forth in Thy service and be con-
nected with Thee by the bonds and ties of Thy
love, longing for the lights of Thy favor. O

Lord! make them signs of guidance, standards of Thy immortal Kingdom, waves of the sea of Thy mercy, mirrors of the light of Thy majesty.

Verily Thou art the Generous! Verily Thou art the Merciful! Verily Thou art the Precious, the Beloved! —*'Abdu'l-Bahá*

37.

O Thou forgiving God! These servants are turning to Thy Kingdom and seeking Thy grace and bounty. O God! Make their hearts good and pure in order that they may become worthy of Thy love. Purify and sanctify the spirits that the light of the Sun of Reality may shine through them. Purify and sanctify the eyes that they may perceive Thy lights. Purify and sanctify the ears in order that they may hear the call of Thy Kingdom. O Lord! Verily we are weak but Thou art mighty. Verily we are poor but Thou art rich. We are seekers and Thou art the one sought. O Lord! have compassion upon us and forgive us; bestow upon us capacity and readiness in order that we may be responsive to Thy favors, attracted to Thy Kingdom, enkindled with the fire of Thy love and resuscitated through the breaths of Thy Holy Spirit in this radiant century. Thou art powerful; Thou art almighty; Thou art merciful; and Thou art most generous! —*'Abdu'l-Bahá*

Morning

38.

I HAVE wakened in Thy shelter, O my God, and it becometh him that seeketh that shelter to abide within the Sanctuary of Thy protection and the Stronghold of Thy defense. Illumine my inner being, O my Lord, with the splendors of the Day-Spring of Thy Revelation, even as Thou didst illumine my outer being with the morning light of Thy favor.   —*Bahá'u'lláh*

39.

I HAVE risen this morning by Thy grace, O my God, and left my home trusting wholly in Thee, and committing myself to Thy care. Send down, then, upon me, out of the heaven of Thy mercy, a blessing from Thy side, and enable me to return home in safety even as Thou didst enable me to set out under Thy protection with my thoughts fixed steadfastly upon Thee.

There is none other God but Thee, the One, the Incomparable, the All-Knowing, the All-Wise. —*Bahá'u'lláh*

40.

I GIVE praise to Thee, O my God, that Thou hast awakened me out of my sleep, and brought me forth after my disappearance, and raised me up from my slumber. I have wakened this morning with my face set toward the splendors of the Day-Star of Thy Revelation, through Which the heavens of Thy power and Thy majesty have been illumined, acknowledging Thy signs, believing in Thy Book, and holding fast unto Thy Cord.

I beseech Thee, by the potency of Thy will and the compelling power of Thy purpose, to make of what Thou didst reveal unto me in my sleep the surest foundation for the mansions of Thy love that are within the hearts of Thy loved ones, and the best instrument for the revelation of the tokens of Thy grace and Thy loving-kindness.

Do Thou ordain for me through Thy most

exalted Pen, O my Lord, the good of this world and of the next. I testify that within Thy grasp are held the reins of all things. Thou changest them as Thou pleasest. No God is there save Thee, the Strong, the Faithful.

Thou art He Who changeth through His bidding abasement into glory, and weakness into strength, and powerlessness into might, and fear into calm, and doubt into certainty. No God is there but Thee, the Mighty, the Beneficent.

Thou disappointest no one who hath sought Thee, nor dost Thou keep back from Thee any one who hath desired Thee. Ordain Thou for me what becometh the heaven of Thy generosity, and the ocean of Thy bounty. Thou art, verily, the Almighty, the Most Powerful.

—Bahá'u'lláh

Praise and Gratitude

MAGNIFIED be Thy Name, O Lord my God!
Thou art He Whom all things worship and
Who worshipeth no one, Who is the Lord of
all things and is the vassal of none, Who knoweth all things and is known of none. Thou didst
wish to make Thyself known unto men; therefore, Thou didst, through a word of Thy mouth,
bring creation into being and fashion the universe. There is none other God except Thee,
the Fashioner, the Creator, the Almighty, the
Most Powerful.

I implore Thee, by this very word that hath
shone forth above the horizon of Thy will, to
enable me to drink deep of the living waters
through which Thou hast vivified the hearts of
Thy chosen ones and quickened the souls of
them that love Thee, that I may, at all times

and under all conditions, turn my face wholly toward Thee.

Thou art the God of power, of glory and bounty. No God is there beside Thee, the Supreme Ruler, the All-Glorious, the Omniscient.
—*Bahá'u'lláh*

42.

ALL PRAISE, O my God, be to Thee Who art the Source of all glory and majesty, of greatness and honor, of sovereignty and dominion, of loftiness and grace, of awe and power. Whomsoever Thou willest Thou causest to draw nigh unto the Most Great Ocean, and on whomsoever Thou desirest Thou conferrest the honor of recognizing Thy Most Ancient Name. Of all who are in heaven and on earth, none can withstand the operation of Thy sovereign Will. From all eternity Thou didst rule the entire creation, and Thou wilt continue for evermore to exercise Thy dominion over all created things. There is none other God but Thee, the Almighty, the Most Exalted, the All-Powerful, the All-Wise.

Illumine, O Lord, the faces of Thy servants, that they may behold Thee; and cleanse their hearts that they may turn unto the court of Thy heavenly favors, and recognize Him Who is the Manifestation of Thy Self and the Day-Spring of Thine Essence. Verily, Thou art the Lord of all worlds. There is no God but Thee, the Unconstrained, the All-Subduing.   —*Bahá'u'lláh*

43·

GLORIFIED art Thou, O Lord my God! I yield Thee thanks for having enabled me to recognize the Manifestation of Thyself, and for having severed me from Thine enemies, and laid bare before mine eyes their misdeeds and wicked works in Thy days, and for having rid me of all attachment to them, and caused me to turn wholly toward Thy grace and bountiful favors. I give Thee thanks, also, for having sent down upon me from the clouds of Thy will that which hath so sanctified me from the hints of the infidels and the allusions of the misbelievers that I have fixed my heart firmly on Thee, and fled from such as have denied the light of Thy countenance. Again I thank Thee for having empowered me to be steadfast in Thy love, and to speak forth Thy praise and to extol Thy virtues, and for having given me to drink of the cup of Thy mercy that hath surpassed all things visible and invisible.

Thou art the Almighty, the Most Exalted, the All-Glorious, the All-Loving.

—Bahá'u'lláh

44.

IN THE NAME of God, the Most High! Lauded and glorified art Thou, Lord, God Omnipotent! Thou before Whose wisdom the wise falleth short and faileth, before Whose knowledge the learned confesseth his ignorance, before Whose might the strong waxeth weak, before Whose wealth the rich testifieth to his poverty, before Whose light the enlightened is lost in darkness, toward the shrine of Whose knowledge turneth the essence of all understanding and around the sanctuary of Whose presence circle the souls of all mankind.

How then can I sing and tell of Thine Essence, which the wisdom of the wise and the learning of the learned have failed to comprehend, inasmuch as no man can sing that which he understandeth not, nor recount that unto which he cannot attain, whilst Thou hast been from everlasting the Inaccessible, the Unsearchable. Powerless though I be to rise to the heavens of Thy glory and soar in the realms of Thy knowledge, I can but recount Thy tokens that tell of Thy glorious handiwork.

By Thy Glory! O Beloved of all hearts, Thou that alone canst still the pangs of yearning for Thee! Though all the dwellers of heaven and earth unite to glorify the least of Thy signs, wherein and whereby Thou hast revealed Thyself, yet would they fail, how much more to praise Thy holy Word, the creator of all Thy tokens.

All praise and glory be to Thee, Thou of Whom all things have testified that Thou art one and there is none other God but Thee, Who hast been from everlasting exalted above all peer or likeness and to everlasting shalt remain the same. All kings are but Thy servants and all beings, visible and invisible, as naught before Thee. There is none other God but Thee, the Gracious, the Powerful, the Most High.

—*'Abdu'l-Bahá*

Prayer for America

45.

O Thou kind Lord! This gathering is turning to Thee. These hearts are radiant with Thy love. These minds and spirits are exhilarated by the message of Thy glad-tidings. O God! Let this American democracy become glorious in spiritual degrees even as it has aspired to material degrees, and render this just government victorious. Confirm this revered nation to upraise the standard of the oneness of humanity, to promulgate the Most Great Peace, to become thereby most glorious and praiseworthy among all the nations of the world. O God! This American nation is worthy of Thy favors and is deserving of Thy mercy. Make it precious and near to Thee through Thy bounty and bestowal.

—'Abdu'l-Bahá

Protection

46.

PRAISED BE Thou, O Lord my God! This is Thy servant who hath quaffed from the hands of Thy grace the wine of Thy tender mercy, and tasted of the savor of Thy love in Thy days. I beseech Thee, by the embodiments of Thy names whom no grief can hinder from rejoicing in Thy love or from gazing on Thy face, and whom all the hosts of the heedless are powerless to cause to turn aside from the path of Thy pleasure, to supply him with the good things Thou dost possess, and to raise him up to such heights that he will regard the world even as a shadow that vanisheth swifter than the twinkling of an eye.

Keep him safe also, O my God, by the power of Thine immeasurable majesty, from all that Thou abhorrest. Thou art, verily, his Lord and the Lord of all worlds.   —*Bahá'u'lláh*

47.

O God, my God! I have set out from my home, holding fast unto the cord of Thy love, and I have committed myself wholly to Thy care and Thy protection. I entreat Thee by Thy power through which Thou didst protect Thy loved ones from the wayward and the perverse, and from every contumacious oppressor, and every wicked doer who hath strayed far from Thee, to keep me safe by Thy bounty and Thy grace. Enable me, then, to return to my home by Thy power and Thy might. Thou art, truly, the Almighty, the Help in Peril, the Self-Subsisting.

—*Bahá'u'lláh*

48.

Praise be to Thee, O Lord my God! Thou seest and knowest that I have called upon Thy servants to turn nowhere except in the direction of Thy bestowals, and have bidden them observe naught save the things Thou didst prescribe in Thy perspicuous Book, the Book which hath been sent down according to Thine inscrutable decree and irrevocable purpose.

I can utter no word, O my God, unless I be

permitted by Thee, and can move in no direction until I obtain Thy sanction. It is Thou, O my God, Who hast called me into being through the power of Thy might, and hast endued me with Thy grace to manifest Thy Cause. Wherefore I have been subjected to such adversities that my tongue hath been hindered from extolling Thee and from magnifying Thy glory.

All praise be to Thee, O my God, for the things Thou didst ordain for me through Thy decree and by the power of Thy sovereignty. I beseech Thee that Thou wilt fortify both myself and them that love me in our love for Thee, and wilt keep us firm in Thy Cause. I swear by Thy might! O my God! Thy servant's shame is to be shut out as by a veil from Thee, and his glory is to know Thee. Armed with the power of Thy Name nothing can ever hurt me, and with Thy love in my heart all the world's afflictions can in no wise alarm me.

Send down, therefore, O my Lord, upon me and upon my loved ones that which will protect us from the mischief of those that have repudiated Thy truth and disbelieved in Thy signs.

Thou art, verily, the All-Glorious, the Most Bountiful.　　　　　　　　　　—*Bahá'u'lláh*

49.

LAUDED BE Thy Name, O Lord my God! I entreat Thee by Thy Name through which the Hour hath struck, and the Resurrection came to pass, and fear and trembling seized all that are in heaven and all that are on earth, to rain down, out of the heaven of Thy mercy and the clouds of Thy tender compassion, what will gladden the hearts of Thy servants, who have turned toward Thee and helped Thy Cause.

Keep safe Thy servants and Thy handmaidens, O my Lord, from the darts of idle fancy and vain imaginings, and give them from the hands of Thy grace a draught of the soft-flowing waters of Thy knowledge.

Thou, truly, art the Almighty, the Most Exalted, the Ever-Forgiving, the Most Generous.

—*Bahá'u'lláh*

50.

O GOD! my God! Shield Thy trusted servants from the evils of self and passion, protect them with the watchful eye of Thy loving-kindness from all rancor, hate and envy, shelter them in the impregnable stronghold of Thy care and, safe from the darts of doubtfulness, make them the manifestations of Thy glorious signs. Illumine their faces with the effulgent rays shed from the Day-Spring of Thy divine Unity, gladden their hearts with the verses revealed from Thy holy Kingdom, strengthen their loins by Thine all-swaying power that cometh from Thy realm of glory. Thou art the All-Bountiful, the Protector, the Almighty, the Gracious!

—'Abdu'l-Bahá

51.

O MY Lord! Thou knowest that the people are encircled with pain and calamities and are environed with hardships and trouble. Every trial doth attack man and every dire adversity doth assail him like unto the assault of a serpent. There is no shelter and asylum for him except under the wing of Thy protection, preservation, guard and custody.

O Thou, the Merciful One! O my Lord! Make Thy protection my armor, Thy preservation my shield, humbleness before the door of Thy oneness my guard, and Thy custody and defense my fortress and my abode. Preserve me from the suggestions of myself and desire, and guard me from every sickness, trial, difficulty and ordeal.

Verily, Thou art the Protector, the Guardian, the Preserver, the Sufficer, and verily, Thou art the Merciful of the Most Merciful!

Abdu'l-Bahá

Severance

52

SUFFER ME, O my God, to draw nigh unto Thee, and to abide within the precincts of Thy court, for remoteness from Thee hath well-nigh consumed me. Cause me to rest under the shadow of the wings of Thy grace, for the flame of my separation from Thee hath melted my heart within me. Draw me nearer unto the river that is life indeed, for my soul burneth with thirst in its ceaseless search after Thee. My sighs, O my God, proclaim the bitterness of mine anguish, and the tears I shed attest my love for Thee.

I beseech Thee, by the praise wherewith Thou praisest Thyself and the glory wherewith Thou glorifiest Thine own Essence, to grant that we may be numbered among them that have recognized Thee and acknowledged Thy sovereignty in Thy days. Help us then to quaff, O my God,

from the fingers of mercy the living waters of
Thy loving-kindness, that we may utterly forget
all else except Thee, and be occupied only with
Thy Self. Powerful art Thou to do what Thou
willest. No God is there beside Thee, the
Mighty, the Help in Peril, the Self-Subsisting.

Glorified be Thy name, O Thou Who art the
King of all Kings!   —*Bahá'u'lláh*

53.

GLORIFIED ART Thou, O my God! I yield Thee
thanks that Thou hast made known unto me
Him Who is the Day-Spring of Thy mercy, and
the Dawning-Place of Thy grace, and the Re-
pository of Thy Cause. I beseech Thee by Thy
Name, through which the faces of them that are
nigh unto Thee have turned white, and the
hearts of such as are devoted to Thee have
winged their flight toward Thee, to grant that
I may, at all times and under all conditions,
lay hold on Thy Cord, and be rid of all attachment to any one except Thee, and may keep
mine eyes directed towards the horizon of Thy
Revelation, and may carry out what Thou hast
prescribed unto me in Thy Tablets.

Attire, O my Lord, both my inner and outer

being with the raiment of Thy favors and Thy loving-kindness. Keep me safe, then, from whatsoever may be abhorrent unto Thee, and graciously assist me and my kindred to obey Thee, and to shun whatsoever may stir up any evil or corrupt desire within me.

Thou, truly, art the Lord of all mankind, and the Possessor of this world and of the next. No God is there save Thee, the All-Knowing, the All-Wise.   —*Bahá'u'lláh*

54.

LAUDED BE Thy Name, O my God! I entreat Thee by the fragrances of the Raiment of Thy grace which at Thy bidding and in conformity with Thy desire were diffused throughout the entire creation, and by the Day-Star of Thy will that hath shone brightly, through the power of Thy might and of Thy sovereignty, above the horizon of Thy mercy, to blot out from my heart all idle fancies and vain imaginings, that with all my affections I may turn unto Thee, O Thou Lord of all mankind!

I am Thy servant and the son of Thy servant, O my God! I have laid hold on the handle of Thy grace, and clung to the cord of Thy tender mercy. Ordain for me the good things that are with Thee, and nourish me from the Table Thou didst send down out of the clouds of Thy bounty and the heaven of Thy favor.

Thou, in very truth, art the Lord of the worlds, and the God of all that are in heaven and all that are on earth.   *—Bahá'u'lláh*

55·

MANY A chilled heart, O my God, hath been set ablaze with the fire of Thy Cause, and many a slumberer hath been wakened by the sweetness of Thy voice. How many are the strangers who have sought shelter beneath the shadow of the tree of Thy oneness, and how numerous the thirsty ones who have panted after the fountain of Thy living waters in Thy days!

Blessed is he that hath set himself towards Thee, and hasted to attain the Day-Spring of the lights of Thy face. Blessed is he who with all his affections hath turned to the Dawning-Place of Thy Revelation and the Fountain-Head of Thine inspiration. Blessed is he that hath expended in Thy path what Thou didst bestow upon him through Thy bounty and favor. Blessed is he who, in his sore longing after

Thee, hath cast away all else except Thyself. Blessed is he who hath enjoyed intimate communion with Thee, and rid himself of all attachment to any one save Thee.

I beseech Thee, O my Lord, by Him Who is Thy Name, Who, through the power of Thy sovereignty and might, hath risen above the horizon of His prison, to ordain for every one what becometh Thee and beseemeth Thine exaltation.

Thy might, in truth, is equal to all things.

—*Bahá'u'lláh*

56.

I KNOW NOT, O my God, what the Fire is which Thou didst kindle in Thy land. Earth can never cloud its splendor, nor water quench its flame. All the peoples of the world are powerless to resist its force. Great is the blessedness of him that hath drawn nigh unto it, and heard its roaring.

Some, O my God, Thou didst, through Thy strengthening grace, enable to approach it, while others Thou didst keep back by reason of what their hands have wrought in Thy days. Whoso hath hasted toward it and attained unto it hath, in his eagerness to gaze on Thy beauty, yielded his life in Thy path, and ascended unto Thee, wholly detached from aught else except Thyself.

I beseech Thee, O my Lord, by this Fire which blazeth and rageth in the world of creation, to rend asunder the veils that have hindered me from appearing before the throne of Thy majesty, and from standing at the door of Thy gate. Do Thou ordain for me, O my Lord, every good thing Thou didst send down in Thy Book, and suffer me not to be far removed from the shelter of Thy mercy.

Powerful art Thou to do what pleaseth Thee. Thou art, verily, the All-Powerful, the Most Generous. —*Bahá'u'lláh*

57.

PRAISE BE unto Thee, O my God! I am one of Thy servants, who hath believed on Thee and on Thy signs. Thou seest how I have set myself toward the door of Thy mercy, and turned my face in the direction of Thy loving-kindness. I beseech Thee, by Thy most excellent titles and Thy most exalted attributes, to open to my face the portals of Thy bestowals. Aid me, then, to do that which is good, O Thou Who art the Possessor of all names and attributes!

I am poor, O my Lord, and Thou art the rich. I have set my face toward Thee, and detached myself from all but Thee. Deprive me not, I implore Thee, of the breezes of Thy tender mercy, and withhold not from me what Thou didst ordain for the chosen among Thy servants.

Remove the veil from mine eyes, O my Lord, that I may recognize what Thou hast desired for Thy creatures, and discover, in all the manifestations of Thy handiwork, the revelations of Thine almighty power. Enrapture my soul, O my Lord, with Thy most mighty signs, and draw me out of the depths of my corrupt and evil desires. Write down, then, for me the good of this world and of the world to come. Potent art Thou to do what pleaseth Thee. No God is there but Thee, the All-Glorious, Whose help is sought by all men.

I yield Thee thanks, O my Lord, that Thou hast wakened me from my sleep, and stirred me up, and created in me the desire to perceive what most of Thy servants have failed to apprehend. Make me able, therefore, O my Lord, to behold, for love of Thee and for the sake of Thy pleasure, whatsoever Thou hast desired. Thou art He to the power of Whose might and sovereignty all things testify.

There is none other God but Thee, the Almighty, the Beneficent.   *—Bahá'u'lláh*

58.

My God! My God! Thou art my Hope and my Beloved, my intended Aim and Desire! With great humbleness and entire devotion I pray to Thee to make me the minaret of Thy love in Thy region, the lamp of Thy knowledge among Thy creatures, and the banner of Thy gift in Thy Kingdom.

Make me one of Thy worshipers who cut themselves from everything but Thee, who sanctify themselves from everything pertaining to the world, and who divert themselves from the defects of the suspicious.

Let my heart be dilated with joy through the spirit of confirmation from Thy Kingdom, and illumine my sight with seeing the hosts of success following one another and descending upon me from Thine Omnipotence.

Thou art the Almighty, the Invincible, the Powerful.   *—'Abdu'l-Bahá*

Spiritual Qualities

59.

CREATE in me a pure heart, O my God, and renew a tranquil conscience within me, O my Hope! Through the spirit of power confirm Thou me in Thy Cause, O my Best-Beloved, and by the light of Thy glory reveal unto me Thy path, O Thou the Goal of my desire! Through the power of Thy transcendent might lift me up unto the heaven of Thy holiness, O Source of my being, and by the breezes of Thine eternity gladden me, O Thou Who art my God! Let Thine everlasting melodies breathe tranquillity on me, O my Companion, and let the riches of Thine ancient countenance deliver me from all except Thee, O my Master, and let the tidings of the revelation of Thine incorruptible Essence bring me joy, O Thou Who art the most manifest of the manifest and the most hidden of the hidden!

—*Bahá'u'lláh*

60.

FROM the sweet-scented streams of Thine eternity give me to drink, O my God, and of the fruits of the tree of Thy being enable me to taste, O my Hope! From the crystal springs of Thy love suffer me to quaff, O my Glory, and beneath the shadow of Thine everlasting providence let me abide, O my Light! Within the meadows of Thy nearness before Thy presence, make me able to roam, O my Beloved, and at the right hand of the throne of Thy mercy, seat me, O my Desire! From the fragrant breezes of Thy joy let a breath pass over me, O my Goal, and into the heights of the paradise of Thy reality let me gain admission, O my Adored One! To the melodies of the dove of Thy oneness suffer me to hearken, O Resplendent One, and through the spirit of Thy power and Thy might quicken me, O my Provider! In the spirit of Thy love keep me steadfast, O my Succorer, and in the path of Thy good-pleasure set firm my steps, O my Maker! Within the garden of Thine immortality, before Thy countenance, let me abide for ever, O Thou Who art merciful unto me, and upon the seat of Thy glory stab-

lish me, O Thou Who art my Possessor! To the
heaven of Thy loving-kindness lift me up, O
my Quickener, and unto the Day-Star of Thy
guidance lead me, O Thou my Attractor! Before the revelations of Thine invisible spirit
summon me to be present, Thou Who art my
Origin and my Highest Wish, and unto the essence of the fragrance of Thy beauty, which
Thou wilt manifest, cause me to return, O
Thou Who art my God!

Potent art Thou to do what pleaseth Thee.
Thou art, verily, the Most Exalted, the All-
Glorious, the All-Highest.   —*Bahá'u'lláh*

61.

O MY LORD! Make Thy beauty to be my food,
and Thy presence my drink, and Thy pleasure
my hope, and praise of Thee my action, and remembrance of Thee my companion, and the
power of Thy sovereignty my succorer, and Thy
habitation my home, and my dwelling-place the
seat Thou hast sanctified from the limitations
imposed upon them who are shut out as by a
veil from Thee.

Thou art, verily, the Almighty, the All-Glorious, the Most Powerful.   —*Bahá'u'lláh*

62.

O MY GOD, the God of bounty and mercy! Thou art that King by Whose commanding word the whole creation hath been called into being; and Thou art that All-Bountiful One the doings of Whose servants have never hindered Him from showing forth His grace, nor have they frustrated the revelations of His bounty.

Suffer this servant, I beseech Thee, to attain unto that which is the cause of his salvation in every world of Thy worlds. Thou art, verily, the Almighty, the Most Powerful, the All-Knowing, the All-Wise.   —*Bahá'u'lláh*

63.

LAUDED BE Thy Name, O Lord my God! I am Thy servant who hath laid hold on the cord of Thy tender mercies, and clung to the hem of Thy bounteousness. I entreat Thee by Thy Name whereby Thou hast subjected all created things, both visible and invisible, and through which the breath that is life indeed was wafted over the entire creation, to strengthen me by Thy power which hath encompassed the heavens and the earth, and to guard me from all sickness and tribulation. I bear witness that Thou art the Lord of all names, and the Ordainer of all that may please Thee. There is none other God but Thee, the Almighty, the All-Knowing, the All-Wise.

Do Thou ordain for me, O my Lord, what will profit me in every world of Thy worlds. Supply me, then, with what Thou hast written down for the chosen ones among Thy creatures, whom neither the blame of the blamer, nor the clamor of the infidel, nor the estrangement of such as have withdrawn from Thee, hath deterred from turning towards Thee.

Thou, truly, art the Help in Peril through the power of Thy sovereignty. No God is there save Thee, the Almighty, the Most Powerful.

—Bahá'u'lláh

64.

O GOD, refresh and gladden my spirit. Purify my heart. Illumine my powers. I lay all my affairs in Thy hand. Thou art my Guide and my Refuge. I will no longer be sorrowful and grieved, I will be a happy and joyful being. O God, I will no longer be full of anxiety, nor will

I let trouble harass me. I will not dwell on the unpleasant things of life.

O God, Thou art more friend to me than I am to myself. I dedicate myself to Thee, O Lord.

—*'Abdu'l-Bahá*

65.

O MY GOD! O my God! Glory be unto Thee for that Thou hast confirmed me to the confession of Thy oneness, attracted me unto the word of Thy singleness, enkindled me by the fire of Thy love, and occupied me with Thy mention and the service of Thy friends and maid-servants.

O Lord, help me to be meek and lowly and strengthen me in severing myself from all things and in holding to the hem of the garment of Thy glory, so that my heart may be filled with Thy love and leave no space for the love of the world and the attachment to its qualities.

O God! Sanctify me from all else save Thee, purge me from the dross of sins and transgressions and cause me to possess a spiritual heart and conscience.

Verily Thou art merciful and, verily, Thou art the Generous, the Helper!   —*'Abdu'l-Bahá*

66.

O MY LORD! O my Lord! This is a lamp lighted by the fire of Thy love and ablaze with the flame which is ignited in the tree of Thy mercy. O my Lord! Increase his enkindlement, heat and flame, with the fire which is kindled in the Sinai of Thy Manifestation. Verily, Thou art the Confirmer, the Assister, the Powerful, the Generous, the Loving!   —*'Abdu'l-Bahá*

67.

O MY GOD! O my God! This, Thy servant, hath advanced toward Thee, is passionately wandering in the desert of Thy love, walking in the path of Thy service, anticipating Thy favors, hoping for Thy bounty, relying upon Thy Kingdom, and being exhilarated with the wine of Thy gift. O my God! Increase his fervor in Thy passion, his constancy in Thy praise and his ardor in Thy love. Verily, Thou art the Beneficent and endowed with great bounty! There is no God but Thee, the Forgiving, the Merciful.   —*'Abdu'l-Bahá*

68.

He is God!

O God, my God! These are servants attracted in Thy days by the fragrances of Thy holiness, enkindled with the flame burning in Thy holy tree, responding to Thy voice, uttering Thy praise, awakened by Thy breeze, stirred by Thy sweet savors, beholding Thy signs, understanding Thy verses, hearkening to Thy words, believing Thy Revelation and assured of Thy loving-kindness. Their eyes, O Lord! are fixed upon Thy Kingdom of effulgent glory and their faces turned toward Thy dominion on high, their hearts beating with the love of Thy radiant and glorious beauty, their souls consumed with the flame of Thy love, O Lord of this world and the world hereafter, their lives seething with the ardor of their longings for Thee and their tears poured forth for Thy sake.

Shield them within the stronghold of Thy protection and safety, preserve them in Thy watchful care, look upon them with the eyes of Thy providence and mercy, make them the signs of Thy divine unity that are manifest throughout all regions, the standards of Thy might that wave above Thy mansions of grandeur, the shining lamps that burn with the oil of Thy wisdom in the globes of Thy guidance, the birds of the garden of Thy knowledge that warble upon the topmost boughs in Thy sheltering paradise and the leviathans of the ocean of Thy bounty that plunge by Thy supreme mercy in the fathomless deeps.

O Lord, my God! Lowly are these servants of Thine, exalt them in Thy Kingdom on high; feeble, strengthen them by Thy supreme power; abased, bestow upon them Thy glory in Thine all-highest realm; poor, enrich them in Thy great dominion. Do Thou then ordain for them all the good Thou hast destined in Thy worlds, visible and invisible, prosper them in this world below, gladden their hearts with Thine inspiration, O Lord of all beings! Illumine their hearts with Thy joyful tidings diffused from Thine all-glorious Station, make firm their steps in Thy Most Great Covenant and strengthen their loins in Thy firm Testament, by Thy bounty and promised grace, O Gracious and Merciful One! Thou art verily the Gracious, the All-Bountiful.

—'Abdu'l-Bahá

69.

HE IS THE Gracious, the All-Bountiful!

O God, my God! Thy Call hath attracted me and the Voice of Thy Pen of Glory awakened me. The stream of Thy holy utterance hath enraptured me and the wine of Thine inspiration entranced me. Thou seest me, O Lord! detached from all things but Thee, clinging to the cord of Thy bounty and craving the wonders of Thy grace. I ask Thee, by the eternal billows of Thy loving-kindness and the shining lights of Thy tender care and favor, to grant that which shall draw me nigh unto Thee and make me rich in Thy wealth. My tongue, my pen, my whole being, testify to Thy power, Thy might, Thy grace and Thy bounty, that Thou art God and there is none other God but Thee, the Powerful, the Mighty.

I bear witness, at this moment, O my God! to my helplessness and Thy sovereignty, my feebleness and Thy power. I know not that which profiteth me or harmeth me; Thou art verily the All-Knowing, the All-Wise. Do Thou decree for me, O Lord, my God, and my Master, that which will make me feel content with Thine eternal decree and will prosper me in every world of Thine. Thou art in truth the Gracious, the Bountiful.

Lord! Turn me not away from the ocean of Thy wealth and the heaven of Thy mercy, and ordain for me the good of this world and hereafter. Verily, Thou art the Lord of the mercy-seat, enthroned in the highest; there is none other God but Thee, the One, the All-Knowing, the All-Wise.   —*'Abdu'l-Bahá*

70.

HE IS THE prayer-hearing, prayer-answering God!

By Thy glory, O Beloved One, Thou giver of light to the world! the flames of separation have consumed me and my waywardness hath melted my heart within me. I ask of Thee, by Thy Most Great Name, O Thou the Desire of the world and the Well-Beloved of mankind! to grant that the breeze of Thine inspiration may sustain my soul, that Thy wondrous voice may reach my ear, that my eyes may behold Thy signs and Thy light as revealed in the manifestations of Thy names and Thine attributes, O Thou within Whose grasp are all things!

Thou seest, O Lord, my God, the tears of Thy favored ones, shed because of their separation from Thee and the fears of Thy devoted ones in their remoteness from Thy Holy Court. By Thy power, that swayeth all things, visible and invisible! It behooveth Thy loved ones to shed tears of blood for that which hath befallen the faithful at the hands of the wicked and the oppressors on the earth. Thou beholdest, O my God! how the ungodly have compassed Thy cities and Thy realms! I ask Thee by Thy Messengers and Thy chosen Ones and by Him whereby the standard of Thy divine unity hath been implanted amidst Thy servants, to shield them by Thy bounty. Thou art, verily, the Gracious, the All-Bountiful.

And, again, I ask Thee by the sweet showers of Thy grace and the billows of the ocean of Thy favor, to ordain for Thy saints that which shall solace their eyes and comfort their hearts. Lord! Thou seest him that kneeleth yearning to arise and serve Thee, the dead calling for eternal life from the ocean of Thy favor and craving to soar to the heavens of Thy wealth, the stranger longing for his home of glory 'neath the canopy of Thy grace, the seeker hastening by Thy mercy to Thy door of bounty, the sinful turning to the ocean of forgiveness and pardon.

By Thy sovereignty, O Thou Who art glorified in the hearts of men, I have turned to Thee, forsaking mine own will and desire, that Thy holy will and pleasure may rule within me and direct me according to that which the pen of Thy eternal decree hath destined for me. This servant, O Lord! though helpless turneth to the Orb of Thy power, though abased hasteneth unto the Day-Spring of glory, though needy craveth the ocean of Thy grace. I beseech Thee by Thy favor and bounty, cast him not away. Thou art verily the Almighty, the Pardoner, the Compassionate. —*'Abdu'l-Bahá*

Steadfastness

71.

GLORIFIED BE Thy Name, O Lord my God! I beseech Thee by Thy power that hath encompassed all created things, and by Thy sovereignty that hath transcended the entire creation, and by Thy Word which was hidden in Thy wisdom and whereby Thou didst create Thy heaven and Thy earth, both to enable us to be steadfast in our love for Thee and in our obedience to Thy pleasure, and to fix our gaze upon Thy face, and celebrate Thy glory. Empower us, then, O my God, to spread abroad Thy signs among Thy creatures, and to guard Thy Faith in Thy realm. Thou hast ever existed independently of the mention of any of Thy creatures, and wilt remain as Thou hast been for ever and ever.

In Thee I have placed my whole confidence, unto Thee I have turned my face, to the cord of

Thy loving providence I have clung, and toward the shadow of Thy mercy I have hastened. Cast me not as one disappointed out of Thy door, O my God, and withhold not from me Thy grace, for Thee alone do I seek. No God is there beside Thee, the Ever-Forgiving, the Most Bountiful.

Praise be to Thee, O Thou Who art the Beloved of them that have known Thee!

—*Bahá'u'lláh*

72.

O THOU Whose nearness is my wish, Whose presence is my hope, Whose remembrance is my desire, Whose court of glory is my goal, Whose abode is my aim, Whose name is my healing, Whose love is the radiance of my heart, Whose service is my highest aspiration! I beseech Thee by Thy Name, through which Thou hast enabled them that have recognized Thee to soar to the sublimest heights of the knowledge of Thee and empowered such as devoutly worship Thee to ascend into the precincts of the court of Thy holy favors, to aid me to turn my face toward Thy face, to fix mine eyes upon Thee, and to speak of Thy glory.

I am the one, O my Lord, who hath forgotten all else but Thee, and turned toward the Day-Spring of Thy grace, who hath forsaken all save Thyself in the hope of drawing nigh unto Thy court. Behold me, then, with mine eyes lifted up toward the Seat that shineth with the splendors of the light of Thy Face. Send down, then, upon me, O my Beloved, that which will enable me to be steadfast in Thy Cause, so that the doubts of the infidels may not hinder me from turning toward Thee.

Thou art, verily, the God of Power, the Help in Peril, the All-Glorious, the Almighty.

—*Bahá'u'lláh*

73.

GLORIFIED art Thou, O Lord my God! I beseech Thee by Him Who is Thy Most Great Name, Who hath been sorely afflicted by such of Thy creatures as have repudiated Thy truth, and Who hath been hemmed in by sorrows which no tongue can describe, to grant that I may remember Thee and celebrate Thy praise, in these days when all have turned away from Thy beauty, have disputed with Thee, and turned away disdainfully from Him Who is the Revealer of Thy Cause. None is there, O my Lord, to help Thee except Thine own Self, and no power to succor Thee save Thine own power.

I entreat Thee to enable me to cleave steadfastly to Thy Love and Thy remembrance. This is, verily, within my power, and Thou art the One that knoweth all that is in me. Thou, in truth, art knowing, apprised of all. Deprive me not, O my Lord, of the splendors of the light of Thy face, whose brightness hath illuminated the whole world. No God is there beside Thee, the Most Powerful, the All-Glorious, the Ever-Forgiving. —*Bahá'u'lláh*

74.

O LORD, my God! Assist Thy loved ones to be firm in Thy Faith, to walk in Thy ways, to be steadfast in Thy Cause. Give them Thy grace to withstand the onslaught of self and passion, to follow the light of Divine Guidance. Thou art the Powerful, the Gracious, the Self-Subsisting, the Bestower, the Compassionate, the Almighty, the All-Bountiful. —*'Abdu'l-Bahá*

75.

MAKE firm our steps, O Lord! in Thy path and strengthen Thou our hearts in Thine obedience. Turn our faces toward the beauty of Thy oneness and gladden our bosoms with the signs of Thy divine unity. Adorn our bodies with the robe of Thy bounty and remove from our eyes the veil of sinfulness and give us the chalice of Thy grace; that the essence of all beings may sing Thy praise before the vision of Thy grandeur. Reveal then Thyself, O Lord! by Thy merciful utterance and the mystery of Thy Divine Being, that the holy ecstacy of prayer may fill our souls—a prayer that shall rise above words and letters and transcend the murmur of syllables and sounds—that all things may be merged into nothingness before the revelation of Thy splendor.

Lord! These are servants that have remained fast and firm in Thy Covenant and Thy Testament, that have held fast unto the cord of constancy in Thy Cause and clung unto the hem of the robe of Thy grandeur. Assist them, O Lord! with Thy grace, confirm with Thy power

and strengthen their loins in obedience to Thee.
Thou art the Pardoner, the Gracious.

—'Abdu'l-Bahá

76.

O God, my God! I have turned in repentance
unto Thee, and verily Thou art the Pardoner,
the Compassionate.

O God, my God! I have returned to Thee,
and verily Thou art the Ever-Forgiving, the
Gracious.

O God, my God! I have clung to the cord of
Thy bounty, and with Thee is the storehouse of
all that is in heaven and earth.

O God, my God! I have hastened toward
Thee, and verily Thou art the Forgiver, the
Lord of grace abounding.

O God, my God! I thirst for the celestial
wine of Thy grace, and verily Thou art the
Giver, the Bountiful, the Gracious, the Almighty.

O God, my God! I testify that Thou hast revealed Thy Cause, fulfilled Thy promise and
sent down from the heaven of Thy grace that
which hath drawn unto Thee the hearts of Thy
favored ones. Well is it with him that hath held

fast unto Thy firm Cord and clung to the hem of Thy resplendent Robe!

I ask Thee, O Lord of all being and King of the seen and unseen, by Thy power, Thy majesty and Thy sovereignty, to grant that my name may be recorded by Thy pen of glory among Thy devoted ones, them whom the scrolls of the sinful hindered not from turning to the Light of Thy countenance, O prayer-hearing, prayer-answering God!

—'Abdu'l-Bahá

77.

O COMPASSIONATE God! Thanks be to Thee for Thou hast awakened and made me conscious. Thou hast given me a seeing eye and favored me with a hearing ear; hast led me to Thy Kingdom and guided me to Thy Path. Thou hast shown me the right way and caused me to enter the Ark of Deliverance. O God! Keep me steadfast and make me firm and staunch. Protect me from violent tests and preserve and shelter me in the strongly fortified fortress of Thy Covenant and Testament. Thou art the Powerful! Thou art the Seeing! Thou art the Hearing! O Thou the Compassionate God!

Bestow upon me a heart which, like unto glass, may be illumined with the light of Thy love, and confer upon me a thought which may change this world into a rose-garden through the spiritual bounty. Thou art the Compassionate, the Merciful! Thou art the Great Beneficent God!

—*'Abdu'l-Bahá*

Teaching

78.

PRAISE BE to Thee, O Lord my God! I implore Thee, by Thy Name which none hath befittingly recognized, and whose import no soul hath fathomed; I beseech Thee, by Him Who is the Fountain-Head of Thy Revelation and the Day-Spring of Thy signs, to make my heart to be a receptacle of Thy love and of remembrance of Thee. Knit it, then, to Thy most great Ocean, that from it may flow out the living waters of Thy wisdom and the crystal streams of Thy glorification and praise.

The limbs of my body testify to Thy unity, and the hair of my head declareth the power of Thy sovereignty and might. I have stood at the door of Thy grace with utter self-effacement and complete abnegation, and clung to the hem of Thy bounty, and fixed mine eyes upon the horizon of Thy gifts.

Do Thou destine for me, O my God, what becometh the greatness of Thy majesty, and assist me, by Thy strengthening grace, so to teach Thy Cause that the dead may speed out of their sepulchers, and rush forth toward Thee, trusting wholly in Thee, and fixing their gaze upon the orient of Thy Cause, and the dawning-place of Thy Revelation.

Thou, verily, art the Most Powerful, the Most High, the All-Knowing, the All-Wise.

—*Bahá'u'lláh*

79.

GLORY BE unto Thee, O Thou God of the world and desire of the nations, O Thou Who hast become manifest in the Greatest Name, whereby the pearls of wisdom and utterance have appeared from the shells of the great sea of Thy knowledge, and the heavens of religions are adorned with the light of the appearance of the sun of Thy countenance!

I beg of Thee—by that Word, by reason of which Thy proof was made perfect among Thy creatures and Thine argument among Thy servants—to strengthen Thy people in that whereby the face of the Cause will radiate in Thy dominion and the standards of Thy power and the banners of Thy guidance will be planted in Thy lands and among Thy servants!

O my God! Thou beholdest them clinging to the rope of Thy grace and holding fast unto the hem of the mantle of Thy beneficence. Ordain for them that which may draw them nearer unto Thee, and withhold them from all else save Thee.

I beg of Thee, O Thou King of existence and protector of the seen and unseen, to make whosoever arises to serve Thy Cause as a sea moving by Thy desire; ablaze with the fire of Thy Sadrat, shining from the horizon of the heaven of Thy will. Verily, Thou art the mighty One, Whom neither the power of all the world, nor the strength of nations can weaken. There is no God but Thee, the One, the Single, the Protector, the Self-Subsistent! —*Bahá'u'lláh*

80.

O GOD, Who art the Author of All Manifestations, the Source of all Sources, the Fountain-Head of all Revelations, and the Well-Spring of all Lights! I testify that by Thy Name the heaven of understanding hath been adorned, and the ocean of utterance hath surged, and the dispensations of Thy providence have been promulgated unto the followers of all religions.

I beseech Thee so to enrich me as to dispense with all save Thee, and be made independent of any one except Thyself. Rain down, then, upon me out of the clouds of Thy bounty that which shall profit me in every world of Thy worlds. Assist me, then, through Thy strengthening grace, so to serve Thy Cause amidst Thy servants that I may show forth what will cause me to be remembered as long as Thine own Kingdom endureth and Thy dominion will last.

This is Thy servant, O my Lord, who with his whole being hath turned unto the horizon of Thy bounty, and the ocean of Thy grace, and the heaven of Thy gifts. Do with me then as becometh Thy majesty, and Thy glory, and Thy bounteousness, and Thy grace.

Thou, in truth, art the God of strength and power, Who art meet to answer them that pray Thee. There is no God save Thee, the All-Knowing, the All-Wise.   —*Bahá'u'lláh*

Tests and Difficulties

81.

DISPEL my grief by Thy bounty and Thy generosity, O God, my God, and banish mine anguish through Thy sovereignty and Thy might. Thou seest me, O my God, with my face set toward Thee at a time when sorrows have compassed me on every side. I implore Thee, O Thou Who art the Lord of all being, and overshadowest all things visible and invisible, by Thy Name whereby Thou hast subdued the hearts and the souls of men, and by the billows of the Ocean of Thy mercy and the splendors of the Day-Star of Thy bounty, to number me with them whom nothing whatsoever hath deterred from setting their faces toward Thee, O Thou Lord of all names and Maker of the heavens.

Thou beholdest, O my Lord, the things which have befallen me in Thy days. I entreat

Thee, by Him who is the Day-Spring of Thy names and the Dawning-Place of Thine attributes, to ordain for me what will enable me to arise to serve Thee and to extol Thy virtues. Thou art, verily, the Almighty, the Most Powerful, Who art wont to answer the prayers of all men!

And, finally, I beg of Thee by the light of Thy countenance to bless my affairs, and redeem my debts, and satisfy my needs. Thou art He to Whose power and to Whose dominion every tongue hath testified, and Whose majesty and Whose sovereignty every understanding heart hath acknowledged. No God is there but Thee, Who hearest and art ready to answer.

—*Bahá'u'lláh*

82.

LAUDED AND glorified art Thou, O my God! I entreat Thee by the sighing of Thy lovers and by the tears shed by them that long to behold Thee, not to withhold from me Thy tender mercies in Thy Day, nor to deprive me of the melodies of the Dove that extolleth Thy oneness before the light that shineth from Thy face. I am the one who is in misery, O God! Behold me cleaving fast to Thy Name, the All-Possessing. I am the one who is sure to perish; behold me clinging to Thy Name, the Imperishable. I implore Thee, therefore, by Thy Self, the Exalted, the Most High, not to abandon me unto mine own self and unto the desires of a corrupt inclination. Hold Thou my hand with the hand of Thy power, and deliver me from the depths of my fancies and idle imaginings, and cleanse me of all that is abhorrent unto Thee.

Cause me, then, to turn wholly unto Thee, to put my whole trust in Thee, to seek Thee as my Refuge, and to flee unto Thy face. Thou art, verily, He Who, through the power of His might, doeth whatsoever He desireth, and commandeth, through the potency of His will, whatsoever He chooseth. None can withstand the operation of Thy decree; none can divert the course of Thine appointment. Thou art, in truth, the Almighty, the All-Glorious, the Most Bountiful.   —Bahá'u'lláh

83.

O THOU Whose tests are a healing medicine to such as are nigh unto Thee, Whose sword is the ardent desire of all them that love Thee, Whose dart is the dearest wish of those hearts that yearn after Thee, Whose decree is the sole hope of them that have recognized Thy truth! I implore Thee, by Thy divine sweetness and by the splendors of the glory of Thy face, to send down upon us from Thy retreats on high that which will enable us to draw nigh unto Thee. Set, then, our feet firm, O my God, in Thy Cause, and enlighten our hearts with the effulgence of Thy knowledge, and illumine our breasts with the brightness of Thy names. *—Bahá'u'lláh*

84.

GLORY TO Thee, O my God! But for the tribulations which are sustained in Thy path, how could Thy true lovers be recognized; and were it not for the trials which are borne for love of Thee, how could the station of such as yearn for Thee be revealed? Thy might beareth me witness! The companions of all who adore Thee are the tears they shed, and the comforters of such as seek Thee are the groans they utter, and the food of them who haste to meet Thee is the fragments of their broken hearts.

How sweet to my taste is the bitterness of death suffered in Thy path, and how precious in my estimation are the shafts of Thine enemies when encountered for the sake of the exaltation of Thy word! Let me quaff in Thy Cause, O my God, whatsoever Thou didst desire, and send down upon me in Thy love all Thou didst ordain. By Thy glory! I wish only what Thou wishest, and cherish what Thou cherishest. In Thee have I, at all times, placed my whole trust and confidence.

Raise up, I implore Thee, O my God, as helpers to this Revelation such as shall be counted worthy of Thy Name and of Thy sovereignty, that they may remember me among Thy creatures, and hoist the ensigns of Thy victory in Thy land.

Potent art Thou to do what pleaseth Thee. No God is there but Thee, the Help in Peril, the Self-Subsisting.   *—Bahá'u'lláh*

85.

GLORIFIED art Thou, O Lord my God! Every man of insight confesseth Thy sovereignty and Thy dominion, and every discerning eye perceiveth the greatness of Thy majesty and the compelling power of Thy might. The winds of tests are powerless to hold back them that enjoy near access to Thee from setting their faces towards the horizon of Thy glory, and the tempests of trials must fail to draw away and hinder such as are wholly devoted to Thy will from approaching Thy court.

Methinks, the lamp of Thy love is burning in their hearts, and the light of Thy tenderness is lit within their breasts. Adversities are incapable of estranging them from Thy Cause, and the vicissitudes of fortune can never cause them to stray from Thy pleasure.

I beseech Thee, O my God, by them and by the sighs which their hearts utter in their separation from Thee, to keep them safe from the mischief of Thine adversaries, and to nourish their souls with what Thou hast ordained for Thy loved ones on whom shall come no fear and who shall not be put to grief.

—Bahá'u'lláh

86.

Is there any Remover of difficulties save God? Say: Praised be God! He is God! All are His servants, and all abide by His bidding!

—The Báb

87.

SAY: God sufficeth all things above all things, and nothing in the heavens or in the earth but God sufficeth. Verily, He is in Himself the Knower, the Sustainer, the Omnipotent.

—*The Báb*

88.

HE IS the Compassionate, the All-Bountiful!

O God, my God! Thou seest me, Thou knowest me; Thou art my Haven and my Refuge. None have I sought nor any will I seek save Thee, no path have I trodden nor any will I tread but the path of Thy love. In the darksome night of despair, my eye turneth expectant and full of hope to the morn of Thy boundless favor and at the hour of dawn my drooping soul is refreshed and strengthened in remembrance of Thy beauty and perfection. He whom the grace of Thy mercy aideth, though he be but a drop, shall become the boundless ocean, and the merest atom which the outpouring of Thy loving-kindness assisteth, shall shine even as the radiant star.

Shelter under Thy protection, O Thou Spirit of purity, Thou Who art the All-Bountiful Provider, this enthralled, enkindled servant of Thine. Aid him in this world of being to remain steadfast and firm in Thy love and grant that this broken-winged bird may attain a refuge and shelter in Thy Divine Nest, that abideth upon the Celestial Tree.   —'Abdu'l-Bahá

89.

O Lord, my God and my Haven in my distress! My Shield and my Shelter in my woes! My Asylum and Refuge in time of need and in my loneliness My Companion! In my anguish my Solace, and in my solitude a loving Friend! The Remover of the pangs of my sorrows and the Pardoner of my sins!

Wholly unto Thee do I turn, fervently imploring Thee with all my heart, my mind and my tongue, to shield me from all that runs counter to Thy will, in this, the cycle of Thy divine unity, and to cleanse me of all defilement that will hinder me from seeking, stainless and unsullied, the shade of the Tree of Thy Grace.

Have mercy, O Lord, on the feeble, make whole the sick, and quench the burning thirst.

Gladden the bosom wherein the fire of Thy love doth smolder and set it aglow with the flame of Thy celestial love and spirit.

Robe the tabernacles of divine unity with the vesture of holiness and set upon my head the crown of Thy favor.

Illumine my face with the radiance of the Orb of Thy bounty and graciously aid me in ministering at Thy Holy Threshold.

Make my heart overflow with love for Thy creatures and grant that I may become the sign of Thy mercy, the token of Thy grace, the promoter of concord amongst Thy loved ones, devoted unto Thee, uttering Thy commemoration and forgetful of self but ever mindful of what is Thine.

O God! My God! Stay not from me the gentle gales of Thy pardon and grace, and deprive me not of the well-springs of Thine aid and favor.

'Neath the shade of Thy protecting wings let me nestle, and cast upon me the glance of Thine all-protecting eye.

Loose my tongue to laud Thy Name amidst Thy people, that my voice may be raised in great assemblies, and from my lips may stream the flood of Thy praise.

Thou art, in all truth, the Gracious, the Glorified, the Mighty, the Omnipotent!

—'Abdu'l-Bahá

90.

O MY Lord, my Beloved, my Desire! Befriend me in my loneliness and accompany me in my exile; remove my sorrow, cause me to be devoted to Thy beauty, withdraw me from all else save Thee, attract me through Thy fragrances of holiness, cause me to be associated in Thy Kingdom with those who are severed from all else save Thee, and who long to serve Thy sacred threshold and who stand to work in Thy Cause. Enable me to be one of Thy maid-servants who have attained to Thy good pleasure. Verily, Thou art the Gracious, the Generous!

—'Abdu'l-Bahá

Unity

91.

O MY God! O my God! Unite the hearts of Thy servants, and reveal to them Thy great purpose. May they follow Thy commandments and abide in Thy law. Help them, O God, in their endeavor, and grant them strength to serve Thee. O God! leave them not to themselves, but guide their steps by the light of knowledge, and cheer their hearts by Thy love. Verily, Thou art their Helper and their Lord.

—*Bahá'u'lláh*

92.

O MY GOD! O my God! Verily I invoke Thee and supplicate before Thy threshold asking Thee that all Thy mercies may descend upon these souls. Specialize them for Thy favor and Thy truth. O Lord! Unite and bind together the hearts, join in accord all the souls and exhilarate the spirits through the signs of Thy sanctity and oneness. O Lord! Make these faces radiant through the light of Thy oneness. Strengthen the loins of Thy servants in the service of Thy kingdom. O Lord, Thou possessor of infinite mercy! O Lord of forgiveness and pardon! Forgive our sins, pardon our shortcomings and cause us to turn to the kingdom of Thy clemency, invoking the kingdom of might and power, humble at Thy shrine and submissive before the glory of Thine evidences. O Lord God! Make us as waves of the sea, as flowers of the garden, united, agreed through the bounties of Thy love. O Lord! Dilate the breasts through the signs of Thy oneness and make all mankind as stars shining from the same height of glory, as perfect fruits growing upon Thy Tree of Life. Verily Thou art the Almighty, the Self-Subsistent, the Giver, the Forgiving, the Pardoner, the Omniscient, the One Creator!

—'Abdu'l-Bahá

BAHÁ'Í OCCASIONAL PRAYERS

Bahá'u'lláh
'Abdu'l-Bahá

TABLE OF CONTENTS

TABLE OF CONTENTS

Obligatory Prayers

"The daily obligatory prayers are three in number . . .
The believer is entirely free to choose any one of those
three prayers, but is under the obligation of reciting either
one of them, and in accordance with any specific directions
with which they may be accompanied."—*Shoghi Effendi*

I.

SHORT OBLIGATORY PRAYER

TO BE RECITED ONCE IN TWENTY-FOUR HOURS,
AT NOON

I BEAR witness, O my God, that Thou hast created me to know Thee and to worship Thee. I
testify, at this moment, to my powerlessness and
to Thy might, to my poverty and to Thy wealth.

There is none other God but Thee, the Help
in Peril, the Self-Subsisting.   —*Bahá'u'lláh*

2.

MEDIUM OBLIGATORY PRAYER

TO BE RECITED DAILY, IN THE MORNING,
AT NOON, AND IN THE EVENING

*Whoso wisheth to pray, let him wash his hands, and
while he washeth, let him say:*

STRENGTHEN my hand, O my God, that it may
take hold of Thy Book with such steadfastness

that the hosts of the world shall have no power over it. Guard it, then, from meddling with whatsoever doth not belong unto it. Thou art, verily, the Almighty, the Most Powerful.

And while washing his face, let him say:

I have turned my face unto Thee, O my Lord! Illumine it with the light of Thy countenance. Protect it, then, from turning to any one but Thee.

Then let him stand up, and facing the Qiblih (point of Adoration, i.e., Bahjí, 'Akká), let him say:

God testifieth that there is none other God but Him. His are the kingdoms of Revelation and of creation. He, in truth, hath manifested Him Who is the Day-Spring of Revelation, Who conversed on Sinai, through Whom the Supreme Horizon hath been made to shine, and the Lote-Tree beyond which there is no passing hath spoken, and through Whom the call hath been proclaimed unto all who are in heaven and on earth: "Lo, the All-Possessing is come. Earth and heaven, glory and dominion are God's, the Lord of all men, and the Possessor of the Throne on high and of earth below!"

Let him, then, bend down, with hands resting on the knees, and say:

Exalted art Thou above my praise and the praise of any one beside me, above my description and the description of all who are in heaven and all who are on earth!

Then, standing with open hands, palms upward toward the face, let him say:

Disappoint not, O my God, him that hath, with beseeching fingers, clung to the hem of Thy mercy and Thy grace, O Thou Who of those who show mercy art the Most Merciful!

Let him, then, be seated and say:

I bear witness to Thy unity and Thy oneness, and that Thou art God, and that there is none other God beside Thee. Thou hast, verily, revealed Thy Cause, fulfilled Thy Covenant, and opened wide the door of Thy grace to all that dwell in heaven and on earth. Blessing and peace, salutation and glory, rest upon Thy loved ones, whom the changes and chances of the world have not deterred from turning unto Thee, and who have given their all, in the hope of obtaining that which is with Thee. Thou art, in truth, the Ever-Forgiving, the All-Bountiful.

If any one choose to recite instead of the long verse these words: "God testifieth that there is none other God but Him, the Help in Peril, the Self-Subsisting," it would be sufficient. And likewise, it would suffice were he, while seated, to choose to recite these words: "I bear witness to Thy unity and Thy oneness, and that Thou art God, and that there is none other God beside Thee."

—Bahá'u'lláh

3.

LONG OBLIGATORY PRAYER

TO BE RECITED ONCE IN TWENTY-FOUR HOURS

Whoso wisheth to recite this prayer, let him stand up and turn unto God, and, as he standeth in his place, let him gaze to the right and to the left, as if awaiting the mercy of his Lord, the Most Merciful, the Compassionate. Then let him say:

O Thou Who art the Lord of all names and the Maker of the heavens! I beseech Thee by them Who are the Day-Springs of Thine invisible Essence, the Most Exalted, the All-Glorious, to make of my prayer a fire that will burn away the veils which have shut me out from Thy beauty, and a light that will lead me unto the ocean of Thy Presence.

Let him then raise his hands in supplication toward God—blessed and exalted be He—and say:

O Thou the Desire of the world and the Beloved of the nations! Thou seest me turning toward Thee, and rid of all attachment to any one save Thee, and clinging to Thy cord, through whose movement the whole creation hath been stirred up. I am Thy servant, O my Lord, and the son of Thy servant. Behold me standing ready to do Thy will and Thy desire, and wishing naught else except Thy good pleasure. I implore Thee by the Ocean of Thy mercy and the Day-Star of Thy grace to do with Thy servant as Thou willest and pleasest. By Thy might which is far above all mention and praise! Whatsoever is revealed by Thee is the desire of my heart and the beloved of my soul. O God, my God! Look not upon my hopes and my doings, nay rather look upon Thy will that hath encompassed the heavens and the earth. By Thy Most Great Name, O Thou Lord of all nations! I have desired only what Thou didst desire, and love only what Thou dost love.

Let him then kneel, and bowing his forehead to the ground, let him say:

Exalted art Thou above the description of any one save Thyself, and the comprehension of aught else except Thee.

Let him then stand and say:

Make my prayer, O my Lord, a fountain of living waters whereby I may live as long as Thy sovereignty endureth, and may make mention of Thee in every world of Thy worlds.

Let him again raise his hands in supplication, and say:

O Thou in separation from Whom hearts and souls have melted, and by the fire of Whose love the whole world hath been set aflame! I implore Thee by Thy Name through which Thou hast subdued the whole creation, not to withhold from me that which is with Thee, O Thou Who rulest over all men! Thou seest, O my Lord, this stranger hastening to his most exalted home beneath the canopy of Thy majesty and within the precincts of Thy mercy; and this transgressor seeking the ocean of Thy forgiveness; and this lowly one the court of Thy glory; and this poor creature the orient of Thy wealth. Thine is the authority to command whatsoever Thou willest. I bear witness that Thou art to be praised in Thy doings, and to be obeyed in Thy behests, and to remain unconstrained in Thy bidding.

Let him then raise his hands, and repeat three times the Greatest Name. Let him then bend down with hands resting on the knees before God—blessed and exalted be He—and say:

Thou seest, O my God, how my spirit hath been stirred up within my limbs and members, in its longing to worship Thee, and in its yearning to remember Thee and extol Thee; how it testifieth to that whereunto the Tongue of Thy Commandment hath testified in the kingdom of Thine utterance and the heaven of Thy knowledge. I love, in this state, O my Lord, to beg of Thee all that is with Thee, that I may demonstrate my poverty, and magnify Thy bounty and Thy riches, and may declare my powerlessness, and manifest Thy power and Thy might.

Let him then stand and raise his hands twice in supplication, and say:

There is no God but Thee, the Almighty, the All-Bountiful. There is no God but Thee, the

Ordainer, both in the beginning and in the end. O God, my God! Thy forgiveness hath emboldened me, and Thy mercy hath strengthened me, and Thy call hath awakened me, and Thy grace hath raised me up and led me unto Thee. Who, otherwise, am I that I should dare to stand at the gate of the city of Thy nearness, or set my face toward the lights that are shining from the heaven of Thy will? Thou seest, O my Lord, this wretched creature knocking at the door of Thy grace, and this evanescent soul seeking the river of everlasting life from the hands of Thy bounty. Thine is the command at all times, O Thou Who art the Lord of all names; and mine is resignation and willing submission to Thy will, O Creator of the heavens!

Let him then raise his hands thrice, and say:

Greater is God than every great one!

Let him then kneel, and bowing his forehead to the ground, say:

Too high art Thou for the praise of those who are nigh unto Thee to ascend unto the heaven of Thy nearness, or for the birds of the hearts of them who are devoted to Thee to attain to the door of Thy gate. I testify that Thou hast

been sanctified above all attributes and holy
above all names. No God is there but Thee,
the Most Exalted, the All-Glorious.

Let him then seat himself and say:

I testify unto that whereunto have testified all
created things, and the Concourse on high, and
the inmates of the all-highest Paradise, and beyond them the Tongue of Grandeur itself from
the all-glorious Horizon, that Thou art God,
that there is no God but Thee, and that He
Who hath been manifested is the Hidden Mystery, the Treasured Symbol, through Whom the
letters B and E (Be) have been joined and knit
together. I testify that it is He Whose name
hath been set down by the Pen of the Most
High, and Who hath been mentioned in the
Books of God, the Lord of the Throne on high
and of earth below.

Let him then stand erect and say:

O Lord of all being and Possessor of all things
visible and invisible! Thou dost perceive my
tears and the sighs I utter, and hearest my groaning, and my wailing, and the lamentation of
my heart. By Thy might! My trespasses have
kept me back from drawing nigh unto Thee;

and my sins have held me far from the court of Thy holiness. Thy love, O my Lord, hath enriched me, and separation from Thee hath destroyed me, and remoteness from Thee hath consumed me. I entreat Thee by Thy footsteps in this wilderness, and by the words "Here am I. Here am I," which Thy chosen Ones have uttered in this immensity, and by the breaths of Thy Revelation, and the gentle winds of the Dawn of Thy Manifestation, to ordain that I may gaze on Thy beauty and observe whatsoever is in Thy Book.

Let him then repeat the Greatest Name thrice, and bend down with hands resting on the knees, and say:

Praise be to Thee, O my God, that Thou hast aided me to remember Thee and to praise Thee, and hast made known unto me Him Who is the Day-Spring of Thy signs, and hast caused me to bow down before Thy Lordship, and humble myself before Thy Godhead, and to acknowledge that which hath been uttered by the Tongue of Thy grandeur.

Let him then rise and say:

O God, my God! My back is bowed by the burden of my sins, and my heedlessness hath destroyed me. Whenever I ponder my evil doings and Thy benevolence, my heart melteth within me, and my blood boileth in my veins. By Thy Beauty, O Thou the Desire of the world! I blush to lift up my face to Thee, and my longing hands are ashamed to stretch forth toward the heaven of Thy bounty. Thou seest, O my God, how my tears prevent me from remembering Thee and from extolling Thy virtues, O Thou the Lord of the Throne on high and of earth below! I implore Thee by the signs of Thy Kingdom and the mysteries of Thy Dominion to do with Thy loved ones as becometh Thy bounty, O Lord of all being, and is worthy of Thy grace, O King of the seen and the unseen!

Let him then repeat the Greatest Name thrice, and kneel with his forehead to the ground, and say:

Praise be unto Thee, O our God, that Thou hast sent down unto us that which draweth us nigh unto Thee, and supplieth us with every good thing sent down by Thee in Thy Books and Thy Scriptures. Protect us, we beseech Thee, O my Lord, from the hosts of idle fancies and vain imaginations. Thou, in truth, art the Mighty, the All-Knowing.

Let him then raise his head, and seat himself, and say:

I testify, O my God, to that whereunto Thy chosen Ones have testified, and acknowledge that which the inmates of the all-highest Paradise and those who have circled round Thy mighty Throne have acknowledged. The kingdoms of earth and heaven are Thine, O Lord of the worlds! —*Bahá'u'lláh*

The Tablet of Aḥmad

4.

"These daily obligatory prayers, together with a few other specific ones, such as the Healing Prayer, the Tablet of Aḥmad, have been invested by Bahá'u'lláh with a special potency and significance, and should therefore be accepted as such and be recited by the believers with unquestioned faith and confidence, that through them they may enter into a much closer communion with God, and identify themselves more fully with His laws and precepts."
—*Shoghi Effendi*

HE IS the King, the All-Knowing, the Wise!

Lo, the Nightingale of Paradise singeth upon the twigs of the Tree of Eternity, with holy and sweet melodies, proclaiming to the sincere ones the glad tidings of the nearness of God, calling the believers in the Divine Unity to the court of the Presence of the Generous One, informing the severed ones of the message which hath been revealed by God, the King, the Glorious, the Peerless, guiding the lovers to the seat of sanctity and to this resplendent Beauty.

Verily this is that Most Great Beauty, foretold in the Books of the Messengers, through Whom truth shall be distinguished from error and the wisdom of every command shall be tested. Verily He is the Tree of Life that bringeth forth the fruits of God, the Exalted, the Powerful, the Great.

O Aḥmad! Bear thou witness that verily He is God and there is no God but Him, the King, the Protector, the Incomparable, the Omnipotent. And that the One Whom He hath sent forth by the name of 'Alí (i.e. His Holiness the Báb) was the true One from God, to Whose commands we are all conforming.

Say: O people be obedient to the ordinances of God, which have been enjoined in the Bayán by the Glorious, the Wise One. Verily He is the King of the Messengers and His Book is the Mother Book did ye but know.

Thus doth the Nightingale utter His call unto you from this prison. He hath but to deliver this clear message. Whosoever desireth, let him turn aside from this counsel and whosoever desireth let him choose the path to his Lord.

O people, if ye deny these verses, by what proof have ye believed in God? Produce it, O assemblage of false ones.

Nay, by the One in Whose hand is my soul, they are not, and never shall be able to do this, even should they combine to assist one another.

O Aḥmad! Forget not My bounties while I am absent. Remember My days during thy days, and My distress and banishment in this remote prison. And be thou so steadfast in My love that thy heart shall not waver, even if the swords of the enemies rain blows upon thee and all the heavens and the earth arise against thee.

Be thou as a flame of fire to My enemies and a river of life eternal to My loved ones, and be not of those who doubt.

And if thou art overtaken by affliction in My path, or degradation for My sake, be not thou troubled thereby.

Rely upon God, thy God and the Lord of thy fathers. For the people are wandering in the paths of delusion, bereft of discernment to see God with their own eyes, or hear His Melody with their own ears. Thus have We found them, as thou also dost witness.

Thus have their superstitions become veils between them and their own hearts and kept them from the path of God, the Exalted, the Great.

Be thou assured in thyself that verily, he who

turns away from this Beauty hath also turned away from the Messengers of the past and showeth pride towards God from all eternity to all eternity.

Learn well this Tablet, O Aḥmad. Chant it during thy days and withhold not thyself therefrom. For verily, God hath ordained for the one who chants it, the reward of a hundred martyrs and a service in both worlds. These favors have We bestowed upon thee as a bounty on Our part and a mercy from Our presence, that thou mayest be of those who are grateful.

By God! Should one who is in affliction or grief read this Tablet with absolute sincerity, God will dispel his sadness, solve his difficulties and remove his afflictions.

Verily, He is the Merciful, the Compassionate. Praise be to God, the Lord of all the worlds.

—*Bahá'u'lláh*

The Tablets of Visitation

5.

(This Tablet is read at the Shrines of Bahá'u'lláh and the Báb. It is also frequently used in commemorating Their anniversaries.)

THE PRAISE which hath dawned from Thy most august Self, and the glory which hath shone forth from Thy most effulgent Beauty, rest upon Thee, O Thou Who art the Manifestation of Grandeur, and the King of Eternity, and the Lord of all who are in heaven and on earth! I testify that through Thee the sovereignty of God and His dominion, and the majesty of God and His grandeur, were revealed, and the Day-Stars of ancient splendor have shed their radiance in the heaven of Thine irrevocable decree, and the Beauty of the Unseen hath shone forth above the horizon of creation. I testify, moreover, that with but a movement of Thy Pen Thine injunction "Be Thou" hath been enforced, and God's hidden Secret hath been divulged, and all created things have been called into being, and all the Revelations have been sent down.

I bear witness, moreover, that through Thy beauty the beauty of the Adored One hath been unveiled, and through Thy face the face of the Desired One hath shone forth, and that through a word from Thee Thou hast decided between all created things, causing them who are devoted to Thee to ascend unto the summit of glory, and the infidels to fall into the lowest abyss.

I bear witness that he who hath known Thee hath known God, and he who hath attained unto Thy presence hath attained unto the presence of God. Great, therefore, is the blessedness of him who hath believed in Thee, and in Thy signs, and hath humbled himself before Thy sovereignty, and hath been honored with meeting Thee, and hath attained the good pleasure of Thy will, and circled around Thee, and stood before Thy throne. Woe betide him that hath transgressed against Thee, and hath denied Thee, and repudiated Thy signs, and gainsaid Thy sovereignty, and risen up against Thee, and waxed proud before Thy face, and hath disputed Thy testimonies, and fled from Thy rule and Thy dominion, and been numbered with the infidels whose names have been inscribed by the fingers of Thy behest upon Thy holy Tablets.

Waft, then, unto me, O my God and my Beloved, from the right hand of Thy mercy and Thy loving-kindness, the holy breaths of Thy favors, that they may draw me away from myself and from the world unto the courts of Thy nearness and Thy presence. Potent art Thou to do what pleaseth Thee. Thou, truly, hast been supreme over all things.

The remembrance of God and His praise, and the glory of God and His splendor, rest upon Thee, O Thou who art His Beauty! I bear witness that the eye of creation hath never gazed upon one wronged like Thee. Thou wast immersed all the days of Thy life beneath an ocean of tribulations. At one time Thou wast in chains and fetters; at another Thou wast threatened by the sword of Thine enemies. Yet, despite all this, Thou didst enjoin upon all men to observe what had been prescribed unto Thee by Him Who is the All-Knowing, the All-Wise.

May my spirit be a sacrifice to the wrongs Thou didst suffer, and my soul be a ransom for the adversities Thou didst sustain. I beseech

God, by Thee and by them whose faces have been illumined with the splendors of the light of Thy countenance, and who, for love of Thee, have observed all whereunto they were bidden, to remove the veils that have come in between Thee and Thy creatures, and to supply me with the good of this world and the world to come. Thou art, in truth, the Almighty, the Most Exalted, the All-Glorious, the Ever-Forgiving, the Most Compassionate.

Bless Thou, O Lord my God, the Divine Lote-Tree and its leaves, and its boughs, and its branches, and its stems, and its offshoots, as long as Thy most excellent titles will endure and Thy most august attributes will last. Protect it, then, from the mischief of the aggressor and the hosts of tyranny. Thou art, in truth, the Almighty, the Most Powerful. Bless Thou, also, O Lord my God, Thy servants and Thy handmaidens who have attained unto Thee. Thou, truly, art the All-Bountiful, Whose grace is infinite. No God is there save Thee, the Ever-Forgiving, the Most Generous. —*Bahá'u'lláh*

6.

(This prayer, revealed by 'Abdu'l-Bahá, is read at His Shrine. It is also used in private prayer.)

Whoso reciteth this prayer with lowliness and fervor will bring gladness and joy to the heart of this Servant: it will be even as meeting Him face to face.

HE IS the All-Glorious!

O God, my God! Lowly and tearful, I raise my suppliant hands to Thee and cover my face in the dust of that Threshold of Thine, exalted above the knowledge of the learned, and the praise of all that glorify Thee. Graciously look upon Thy servant, humble and lowly at Thy door, with the glances of the eye of Thy mercy, and immerse him in the Ocean of Thine eternal grace.

Lord! He is a poor and lowly servant of Thine, enthralled and imploring Thee, captive in Thy hand, praying fervently to Thee, trusting in Thee, in tears before Thy face, calling to Thee and beseeching Thee, saying:

O Lord, my God! Give me Thy grace to serve Thy loved ones, strengthen me in my servitude to Thee, illumine my brow with the light of adoration in Thy court of holiness, and of prayer to Thy Kingdom of grandeur. Help me to be selfless at the heavenly entrance of Thy gate, and aid me to be detached from all things within Thy holy precincts. Lord! Give me to drink from the chalice of selflessness; with its robe clothe me, and in its ocean immerse me. Make me as dust in the pathway of Thy loved ones, and grant that I may offer up my soul for the earth ennobled by the footsteps of Thy chosen ones in Thy path, O Lord of Glory in the Highest.

With this prayer doth Thy servant call Thee, at dawn-tide and in the night-season. Fulfill his heart's desire, O Lord! Illumine his heart, gladden his bosom, kindle his light, that he may serve Thy Cause and Thy servants.

Thou art the Bestower, the Pitiful, the Most Bountiful, the Gracious, the Merciful, the Compassionate!   —'Abdu'l-Bahá

Firmness in the Covenant

7.

GLORY BE to Thee, O King of eternity, and the Maker of nations, and the Fashioner of every moldering bone! I pray Thee, by Thy Name through which Thou didst call all mankind unto the horizon of Thy majesty and glory, and didst guide Thy servants to the court of Thy grace and favors, to number me with such as have rid themselves from everything except Thyself, and have set themselves towards Thee, and have not been kept back by such misfortunes as were decreed by Thee, from turning in the direction of Thy gifts.

I have laid hold, O my Lord, on the handle of Thy bounty, and clung steadfastly to the hem of the robe of Thy favor. Send down, then, upon me, out of the clouds of Thy generosity, what will purge out from me the remembrance of any one except Thee, and make me able to turn unto Him Who is the Object of the adoration of all mankind, against Whom have been arrayed the stirrers of sedition, who have broken Thy covenant, and disbelieved in Thee and in Thy signs.

Deny me not, O my Lord, the fragrances of Thy raiment in Thy days, and deprive me not of the breathings of Thy Revelation at the appearance of the splendors of the light of Thy face. Powerful art Thou to do what pleaseth Thee. Naught can resist Thy will, nor frustrate what Thou hast purposed by Thy power.

No God is there but Thee, the Almighty, the All-Wise.   —*Bahá'u'lláh*

8.

HE IS the Mighty! the Pardoner! the Compassionate!

O God, my God! Thou beholdest Thy servants in the abyss of perdition and error; where is Thy light of divine guidance, O Thou the Desire of the world? Thou knowest their helplessness and their feebleness; where is Thy power, O Thou in Whose grasp lay the powers of heaven and earth?

I ask Thee, O Lord! my God, by the splendor of the lights of Thy loving-kindness and the billows of the ocean of Thy knowledge and wisdom and by Thy Word wherewith Thou hast swayed the peoples of Thy dominion, to grant that I may be one of them that have observed Thy bidding in Thy Book. And do Thou ordain for me that which Thou hast ordained for Thy trusted ones, them that have quaffed the wine of divine inspiration from the chalice of Thy bounty and hastened to do Thy pleasure and observe Thy Covenant and Testament. Powerful art Thou to do as Thou willest, there is none other God but Thee, the All-Knowing, the All-Wise.

Decree for me, by Thy bounty, O Lord! that which shall prosper me in this world and hereafter and shall draw me nigh unto Thee, O Thou Who art the Lord of all men; there is none other God but Thee, the One, the Mighty, the Glorified.   —'Abdu'l-Bahá

Prayers for Teaching

FROM THE TABLETS OF THE DIVINE PLAN
REVEALED BY 'ABDU'L-BAHÁ

9.

O THOU incomparable God! O Thou Lord of the Kingdom! These souls are Thy heavenly army. Assist them and with the cohorts of the Supreme Concourse, make them victorious; so that each one of them may become like unto a regiment and conquer these countries through the love of God and the illumination of divine teachings.

O God! Be Thou their supporter and their helper, and in the wilderness, the mountain, the valley, the forests, the prairies and the seas, be Thou their confidant—so that they may cry out through the power of the Kingdom and the breath of the Holy Spirit!

Verily Thou art the Powerful, the Mighty and the Omnipotent, and Thou art the Wise, the Hearing and the Seeing.

10.

Any soul starting on a trip of teaching to various parts, and while sojourning in strange countries, may peruse the following supplication—day and night:

O God! O God! Thou seest me enamored and attracted toward Thy Kingdom, the El-Abhá, enkindled with the fire of Thy love amongst mankind, a herald of Thy Kingdom in these vast and spacious countries, severed from aught else save Thee, relying on Thee, abandoning rest and comfort, remote from my native home, a wanderer in these regions, a stranger fallen on the ground, humble before Thy exalted threshold, submissive toward Thy most high realm, supplicating Thee in the middle of nights and in the heart of evenings, entreating and invoking Thee in the morn and eve—so that Thou mayest assist me in the service of Thy Cause, the promotion of Thy Teachings and the exaltation of Thy Word in the easts of the earth and the wests thereof.

O Lord! Strengthen my back and confirm me in Thy servitude with all my powers, and do not leave me alone and by myself in these countries.

O Lord! Associate with me in my loneliness

and accompany me in my journeys through these foreign lands.

Verily, Thou art the confirmer of whomsoever Thou willest in that which Thou desirest, and verily Thou art the Powerful, the Omnipotent.

II.

Let whosoever travels to different parts to teach, peruse over mountain, desert, land and sea this supplication!

O God! O God! Thou seest my weakness, lowliness and humility before Thy creatures; nevertheless, I have trusted in Thee and have arisen in the promotion of Thy teachings among Thy strong servants, relying on Thy power and might.

O Lord! I am a broken-winged bird and desire to soar in Thy limitless space. How is it possible for me to do this save through Thy providence and grace, Thy confirmation and assistance.

O Lord have pity on my weakness and strengthen me with Thy power! O Lord, have pity on my impotence and assist me with Thy might and majesty!

O Lord! Should the breath of the Holy Spirit

confirm the weakest of creatures, he would attain all to which he aspireth and would possess anything he desireth. Indeed Thou hast assisted Thy servants in the past, and though they were the weakest of Thy creatures, the lowliest of Thy servants and the most insignificant of those who lived upon the earth, through Thy sanction and potency they took precedence over the most glorious of Thy people and the most noble of mankind. Whereas formerly they were as moths, they became as royal falcons, and whereas before they were as brooks, they became as seas, through Thy bestowal and Thy mercy. They became through Thy most great favor stars shining on the horizon of guidance, birds singing in the rose-gardens of immortality, lions roaring in the forests of knowledge and wisdom, and whales swimming in the oceans of life.

Verily, Thou art the Clement, the Powerful, the Mighty, and the Most Merciful of the Merciful!

12.

O GOD! O GOD! Thou seest that black darkness hath encompassed all the regions, all the countries are burning with the conflagration of dissension and the fire of war and carnage is ignited in the easts of the earth and the wests thereof. The blood is being shed, the corpses are outstretched and the heads are decapitated and thrown on the ground in the battlefield.

Lord! Lord! Have pity on these ignorant ones, look upon them with the eye of forgiveness and pardon. Extinguish this fire so that these gloomy clouds covering the horizon may be scattered; the Sun of Reality may shine forth with the rays of conciliation; this darkness be rent asunder and all the countries be illumined with the lights of peace.

Lord! Awaken them from the depths of the sea of animosity, deliver them from these impenetrable darknesses, establish affinity between their hearts and enlighten their eyes with the light of peace and reconciliation.

Lord! Rescue them from the fathomless depths of war and bloodshed! Arouse them out of the gloom of error, rend asunder the veil from their eyes, brighten their hearts with the light of guidance, deal with them through Thy favor and mercy and do not treat them according to Thy justice and wrath through which the backs of the mighty ones are shaken!

Lord! Verily the wars have prolonged, the calamities have increased, and every building hath turned into ruin.

Lord! Verily the breasts are agitated and the souls are convulsed. Have mercy on these poor ones and do not leave them to do with themselves that which they desire!

Lord! Send forth throughout Thy countries humble and submissive souls, their faces illumined with the rays of guidance, severed from the world, speaking Thy remembrance and praise and diffusing Thy holy fragrances amongst mankind!

Lord! Strengthen their backs, reinforce their loins and dilate their breasts with the signs of Thy most great love.

Lord! Verily they are weak and Thou art the Powerful and the Mighty; and they are impotent and Thou art the Helper and the Merciful!

Lord! Verily the sea of transgression is waving high and these hurricanes will not be calmed down save through Thy boundless grace which hath embraced all the regions!

Lord! Verily the souls are in the deep valleys of lust and nothing will awaken them save Thy most wonderful bounties.

Lord! Dispel these darknesses of temptations

and illumine the hearts with the lamp of Thy love, through which all the countries will be enlightened. Confirm those believers who, leaving their countries, their families and their children, travel throughout the regions for the sake of the love of Thy beauty, the diffusion of Thy fragrances and the promulgation of Thy teachings. Be thou their companion in their loneliness, their helper in a strange land, the remover of their sorrow, the comforter in their calamity, their deliverer in their hardship, the satisfier of their thirst, the healer of their malady and the allayer of the fire of their longing.

Verily, Thou art the Clement, the Possessor of Mercy, and verily Thou art the Compassionate and the Merciful.

13.

The following supplication is to be read by the teachers and friends daily:

O Thou kind Lord! Praise be unto Thee that Thou hast shown us the highway of guidance, opened the doors of the kingdom and manifested Thyself through the Sun of Reality. To the blind Thou hast given sight; to the deaf Thou hast granted hearing; Thou hast resuscitated the dead; Thou hast enriched the poor; Thou hast shown the way to those who have gone astray; Thou hast led those with parched lips to the fountain of guidance; Thou hast suffered the thirsty fish to reach the ocean of reality and Thou hast invited the wandering birds to the rose-garden of grace.

O Thou Almighty! We are Thy servants and Thy poor ones; we are remote and yearn for Thy presence; are athirst for the water of Thy fountain; are ill, longing for Thy healing. We are walking in Thy path and have no aim or hope save the diffusion of Thy fragrance, so that all souls raise the cry of "O God, guide us to the straight path". May their eyes be opened to behold the light, and may they be freed from the darkness of ignorance. May they gather around the lamp of Thy guidance. May every portionless one receive a share. May the deprived ones become the confidants of Thy mysteries.

O Almighty! Look upon us with the glance of mercifulness. Grant us heavenly confirmation. Bestow upon us the breath of the Holy Spirit, so that we may be assisted in Thy service and like unto brilliant stars, shine in these regions with the light of Thy guidance.

Verily, Thou art the Powerful, the Mighty, the Wise and the Seeing.

(Revealed to the Bahá'ís
of the Northeastern States)

14.

Every soul who travels through these cities, villages and hamlets of these States and is engaged in the diffusion of the fragrances of God, must peruse this commune every morning:

O my God! O my God! Thou seest me in my lowliness and weakness, occupied with the greatest undertaking, determined to raise Thy word among the masses and to spread Thy teachings among Thy peoples. How can I succeed unless Thou assist me with the breath of the Holy Spirit, help me to triumph by the hosts of Thy glorious Kingdom, and shower upon me Thy confirmations which alone can change a gnat into an eagle, a drop of water into rivers and seas, and an atom into lights and suns? O my Lord! Assist me with Thy triumphant and effective might, so that my tongue may utter Thy praises and attributes among all people and my soul overflow with the wine of Thy love and knowledge.

Thou art the Omnipotent and the Doer of whatsoever Thou willest!

(Revealed to the Bahá'ís of the Southern States)

15.

The spreaders of the fragrances of God may peruse this commune every morning:

O Lord! O Lord! Praise and thanksgiving be unto Thee for Thou hast guided me to the highway of the Kingdom, suffered me to walk in this straight and far-stretching path, illumined my eye by beholding the lights, made me listen to the melodies of the birds of holiness from the Kingdom of Mysteries and attracted my heart with Thy love among the righteous.

O Lord! Confirm me with the Holy Spirit, so that I may call in Thy Name amongst the nations and give the glad tidings of the manifestation of Thy Kingdom amongst mankind.

O Lord! I am weak, strengthen me with Thy power and potency. My tongue falters, suffer me to utter Thy commemoration and praise. I am lowly, honor me through my entrance into Thy Kingdom. I am remote, cause me to approach the threshold of Thy mercifulness. O Lord! Make me a brilliant lamp, a shining star and a blessed tree, adorned with fruit, its branches overshadowing all these regions! Verily, Thou art the Mighty, the Powerful and Unconstrained!

(Revealed to the Bahá'ís of the Central States)

16.

The following commune is to be read . . . every day:

O GOD! O God! This is a broken-winged bird and his flight is very slow—assist him so that he may fly toward the apex of prosperity and salvation, wing his way with the utmost joy and happiness throughout the illimitable space, raise his melody in Thy Supreme Name in all the regions, exhilarate the ears with this call, and brighten the eyes by beholding the signs of guidance!

O Lord! I am single, alone and lowly. For me there is no support save Thee, no helper except Thee and no sustainer beside Thee. Confirm me in Thy service, assist me with the cohorts of

Thy angels, make me victorious in the promotion of Thy Word and suffer me to speak out Thy wisdom amongst Thy creatures. Verily, Thou art the custodian of the poor and the defender of the little ones, and verily Thou art the Powerful, the Mighty and the Unconstrained!

(Revealed to the Bahá'ís
of the Western States)

17.

The spreaders of the fragrances of God should peruse every morning the following supplication:

PRAISE be to Thee, O God! Verily, these are Thy servants, who are attracted by the fragrances of Thy mercifulness, enkindled by the ignited fire in the tree of Thy singleness, and their eyes are brightened by beholding the effulgences of the light in the Sinai of Thy oneness!

O Lord! Loosen their tongues in Thy commemoration amongst Thy people; suffer them to speak Thy praise through Thy favor and grace, assist them with the cohorts of Thine angels, strengthen their loins in Thy service and make them the signs of Thy guidance amongst Thy creatures!

Verily, Thou art the Powerful, the Exalted, the Pardoner and the Merciful!

O God! O God! Thou beholdest this weak one begging the strength of Thy Kingdom! This poor one supplicating the treasures of Thy heaven! This thirsty one longing for Thy fountain of the water of eternal life! This sick one invoking Thy perfect recovery through Thy boundless mercy, which Thou hast specialized for Thy chosen servants in Thy Supreme Kingdom!

O Lord! I have no other helper save Thee, no other comforter beside Thee, and no other sustainer except Thee! Assist me with Thine angels in the diffusion of Thy holy fragrances and the dissemination of Thy teachings amongst Thine elected people!

O Lord! Suffer me to sever myself from aught else save Thee, holding fast to the hem of Thy garment; make me sincere in Thy religion, firm in Thy love and living in accordance with that which Thou hast commanded me in Thy Book.

Verily, Thou art the Powerful, the Mighty and the Omnipotent! (Revealed to the Bahá'ís of Canada)

Spiritual Assembly

18.

Whenever ye enter the council chamber, recite this prayer with a heart throbbing with the love of God and a tongue purified from all but His remembrance, that the All-Powerful may graciously aid you to achieve supreme victory.

O God! my God! We are servants of Thine that have turned with devotion to Thy holy face, that have detached ourselves from all beside Thee in this glorious Day. We have gathered in this spiritual assembly, united in our views and thoughts, with our purposes harmonized to exalt Thy Word amidst mankind. O Lord, our God! Make us the signs of Thy divine guidance, the standards of Thine exalted Faith amongst men, servants to Thy mighty Covenant, O Thou our Lord Most High, manifestations of Thy divine unity in Thine Abhá Kingdom, and resplendent stars shining upon all regions. Lord! Aid us to become seas surging with the billows of Thy wondrous grace, streams flowing from Thine all-glorious heights, goodly fruits upon the tree of Thy heavenly Cause, trees waving through the breezes of Thy bounty in Thy celestial vineyard. O God! Make our souls dependent upon the verses of Thy divine unity, our hearts cheered with the outpourings of Thy grace, that we may unite even as the waves of one sea and become merged together as the rays of Thine effulgent light; that our thoughts, our views, our feelings may become as one reality, manifesting the spirit of union throughout the world. Thou art the Gracious, the Bountiful, the Bestower, the Almighty, the Merciful, the Compassionate. —'Abdu'l-Bahá

19.

Prayer to be said at the close of the meeting of the House of Spirituality [Spiritual Assembly].

O God! O God! Thou dost look upon us from Thine unseen Kingdom of oneness, beholding that we have assembled in this spiritual meeting, believing in Thee, confident in Thy signs, firm in Thy Covenant and Testament, attracted unto Thee, set aglow with the fire of Thy love, sincere in Thy Cause, servants in Thy vineyard, spreaders of Thy religion, worshipers of Thy countenance, humble to Thy Beloved, submissive at Thy door and imploring Thee to confirm us in the service of Thy chosen ones. Support us with Thine unseen hosts, strengthen our loins in Thy servitude and make us submissive and worshiping servants, communing with Thee.

O our Lord! We are weak and Thou art the Mighty, the Powerful! We are mortals and Thou art the great life-giving Spirit! We are needy and Thou art the Powerful and Sustainer!

O our Lord! Turn our faces unto Thy divine face; feed us from Thy heavenly table by Thy godly grace; help us through the hosts of Thy supreme angels and confirm us by the holy ones of the Kingdom of Abhá.

Verily, Thou art the Generous, the Merciful! Thou art possessor of great bounty and verily, Thou art the Clement and Gracious!

—'Abdu'l-Bahá

Intercalary Days

(The Intercalary Days, February 26 to March 1, inclusive, should be days of preparation for the Fast, days of hospitality, charity and the giving of presents.)

20.

MY GOD, my Fire and my Light! The days which Thou hast named the Ayyám-i-Há (the Days of Há, Intercalary days) in Thy Book have begun, O Thou Who art the King of names, and the fast which Thy most exalted Pen hath enjoined unto all who are in the kingdom of Thy creation to observe is approaching. I entreat Thee, O my Lord, by these days and by all such as have during that period clung to the cord of Thy commandments, and laid hold on the handle of Thy precepts, to grant that unto every soul may be assigned a place within the precincts of Thy court, and a seat at the revelation of the splendors of the light of Thy countenance.

These, O my Lord, are Thy servants whom no corrupt inclination hath kept back from what Thou didst send down in Thy Book. They have bowed themselves before Thy Cause, and received Thy Book with such resolve as is born of Thee, and observed what Thou hadst prescribed unto them, and chosen to follow that which had been sent down by Thee.

Thou seest, O my Lord, how they have recognized and confessed whatsoever Thou hast revealed in Thy Scriptures. Give them to drink, O my Lord, from the hands of Thy graciousness the waters of Thine eternity. Write down, then, for them the recompense ordained for him that hath immersed himself in the ocean of Thy presence, and attained unto the choice wine of Thy meeting.

I implore Thee, O Thou the King of kings and the Pitier of the downtrodden, to ordain for them the good of this world and of the world to come. Write down for them, moreover, what none of Thy creatures hath discovered and number them with those who have circled round Thee, and who move about Thy throne in every world of Thy worlds.

Thou, truly, art the Almighty, the All-Knowing, the All-Informed.   —*Bahá'u'lláh*

The Fast

The *Aqdas* states: *"We have commanded you to pray and fast from the beginning of maturity* [15 years]; *this is ordained by God, your Lord and the Lord of your forefathers. . . . The traveler, the ailing, those who are with child or giving suck, are not bound by the fast. . . . Abstain from food and drink, from sunrise to sundown, and beware lest desire deprive you of this grace that is appointed in the Book."*

The period of the Fast is March 2 through March 20.

21.

I BESEECH Thee, O my God, by Thy mighty Sign, and by the revelation of Thy grace amongst men, to cast me not away from the gate of the city of Thy presence, and to disappoint not the hopes I have set on the manifestations of Thy grace amidst Thy creatures. Thou seest me, O my God, holding to Thy Name, the Most Holy, the Most Luminous, the Most Mighty, the Most Great, the Most Exalted, the Most Glorious and clinging to the hem of the robe to which have clung all in this world and in the world to come.

I beseech Thee, O my God, by Thy most sweet Voice and by Thy most exalted Word, to draw me ever nearer to the threshold of Thy door, and to suffer me not to be far removed from the shadow of Thy mercy and the canopy of Thy bounty. Thou seest me, O my God, holding to Thy Name, the Most Holy, the Most Luminous, the Most Mighty, the Most Great, the Most Exalted, the Most Glorious, and clinging to the hem of the robe to which have clung all in this world and in the world to come.

I beseech Thee, O my God, by the splendor of Thy luminous brow and the brightness of the light of Thy countenance, which shineth from the all-highest horizon, to attract me by the fragrance of Thy raiment, and make me drink of the choice wine of Thine utterance. Thou seest me, O my God, holding to Thy Name, the Most Holy, the Most Luminous, the Most Mighty, the Most Great, the Most Exalted, the Most Glorious, and clinging to the hem of the robe to which have clung all in this world and in the world to come.

I beseech Thee, O my God, by Thy hair which moveth across Thy face, even as Thy most exalted pen moveth across the pages of Thy Tablets, shedding the musk of hidden meanings over the kingdom of Thy creation, so to raise me up to serve Thy Cause that I shall not fall back, nor be hindered by the suggestions of them who have caviled at Thy signs and turned away from Thy face. Thou seest me, O my God, holding to Thy Name, the Most Holy, the Most Luminous, the Most Mighty, the Most Great, the Most Exalted, the Most Glorious, and clinging to the hem of the robe to which have clung all in this world and in the world to come.

I beseech Thee, O my God, by Thy Name which Thou hast made the King of Names, by which all who are in heaven and all who are on earth have been enraptured, to enable me to gaze on the Day-Star of Thy Beauty, and to supply me with the wine of Thine utterance. Thou seest me, O my God, holding to Thy Name, the Most Holy, the Most Luminous, the Most Mighty, the Most Great, the Most Exalted, the Most Glorious, and clinging to the hem of the robe to which have clung all in this world and in the world to come.

I beseech Thee, O my God, by the Tabernacle of Thy majesty upon the loftiest summits, and the Canopy of Thy Revelation on the highest hills, to graciously aid me to do what Thy will hath desired and Thy purpose hath manifested. Thou seest me, O my God, holding to Thy Name, the Most Holy, the Most Luminous, the Most Mighty, the Most Great, the Most Exalted, the Most Glorious, and clinging to the hem of the robe to which have clung all in this world and in the world to come.

I beseech Thee, O my God, by Thy Beauty that shineth forth above the horizon of eternity, a Beauty before which as soon as it revealeth itself the kingdom of beauty boweth down in worship, magnifying it in ringing tones, to grant that I may die to all that I possess and live to whatsoever belongeth unto Thee. Thou seest me, O my God, holding to Thy Name, the Most Holy, the Most Luminous, the Most Mighty, the Most Great, the Most Exalted, the Most Glorious, and clinging to the hem of the robe to which have clung all in this world and in the world to come.

I beseech Thee, O my God, by the Manifestation of Thy Name, the Well-Beloved, through Whom the hearts of Thy lovers were consumed and the souls of all that dwell on earth have soared aloft, to aid me to remember Thee amongst Thy creatures, and to extol Thee amidst Thy people. Thou seest me, O my God, holding to Thy Name, the Most Holy, the Most Luminous, the Most Mighty, the Most Great, the Most Exalted, the Most Glorious, and clinging to the hem of the robe to which have clung all in this world and in the world to come.

I beseech Thee, O my God, by the rustling of the Divine Lote-Tree and the murmur of the breezes of Thine utterance in the kingdom of Thy names, to remove me far from whatsoever Thy will abhorreth, and draw me nigh unto the station wherein He Who is the Day-Spring of Thy signs hath shone forth. Thou seest me, O my God, holding to Thy Name, the Most Holy, the Most Luminous, the Most Mighty, the Most Great, the Most Exalted, the Most Glorious, and clinging to the hem of the robe to which have clung all in this world and in the world to come.

I beseech Thee, O my God, by that Letter which, as soon as it proceeded out of the mouth of Thy will, hath caused the oceans to surge, and the winds to blow, and the fruits to be revealed, and the trees to spring forth, and all past traces to vanish, and all veils to be rent asunder, and them who are devoted to Thee to hasten unto the light of the countenance of their Lord, the Unconstrained, to make known unto me what lay hid in the treasuries of Thy knowledge and concealed within the repositories of Thy wisdom. Thou seest me, O my God, holding to Thy Name, the Most Holy, the Most Luminous, the Most Mighty, the Most Great, the Most Exalted, the Most Glorious, and clinging to the hem of the robe to which have clung all in this world and in the world to come.

I beseech Thee, O my God, by the fire of Thy Love which drove sleep from the eyes of Thy chosen ones and Thy loved ones, and by their remembrance and praise of Thee at the hour of dawn, to number me with such as have attained unto that which Thou hast sent down in Thy Book and manifested through Thy will. Thou seest me, O my God, holding to Thy Name, the Most Holy, the Most Luminous, the Most Mighty, the Most Great, the Most Exalted, the Most Glorious, and clinging to the hem of the robe to which have clung all in this world and in the world to come.

I beseech Thee, O my God, by the light of Thy countenance which impelled them who are nigh unto Thee to meet the darts of Thy decree, and such as are devoted to Thee to face the swords of Thine enemies in Thy path, to write down for me with Thy most exalted Pen what Thou hast written down for Thy trusted ones and Thy chosen ones. Thou seest me, O my God, holding to Thy Name, the Most Holy, the Most Luminous, the Most Mighty, the Most Great, the Most Exalted, the Most Glorious, and clinging to the hem of the robe to which have clung all in this world and in the world to come.

I beseech Thee, O my God, by Thy Name through which Thou hast hearkened unto the call of Thy lovers, and the sighs of them that long for Thee, and the cry of them that enjoy near access to Thee, and the groaning of them that are devoted to Thee, and through which Thou hast fulfilled the wishes of them that have set their hopes on Thee, and hast granted them their desires, through Thy grace and Thy favors, and by Thy Name through which the ocean of forgiveness surged before Thy face, and the clouds of Thy generosity rained upon Thy serv-ants, to write down for every one who hath turned unto Thee, and observed the fast pre-scribed by Thee, the recompense decreed for such as speak not except by Thy leave, and who forsook all that they possessed in Thy path and for love of Thee.

I beseech Thee, O my Lord, by Thyself, and by Thy signs, and Thy clear tokens, and the shining light of the Day-Star of Thy Beauty, and Thy Branches, to cancel the trespasses of those who have held fast to Thy laws, and have observed what Thou hast prescribed unto them in Thy Book. Thou seest me, O my God, holding to Thy Name, the Most Holy, the Most Luminous, the Most Mighty, the Most Great, the Most Exalted, the Most Glorious, and clinging to the hem of the robe to which have clung all in this world and in the world to come.

—*Bahá'u'lláh*

22.

PRAISE be to Thee, O Lord my God! I beseech Thee by this Revelation whereby darkness hath been turned into light, through which the Frequented Fane hath been built, and the Written Tablet revealed, and the Outspread Roll uncovered, to send down upon me and upon them who are in my company that which will enable us to soar into the heavens of Thy transcendent glory, and will wash us from the stain of such doubts as have hindered the suspicious from entering into the tabernacle of Thy unity.

I am the one, O my Lord, who hath held fast the cord of Thy loving-kindness, and clung to the hem of Thy mercy and favors. Do Thou ordain for me and for my loved ones the good of this world and of the world to come. Supply them, then, with the Hidden Gift Thou didst ordain for the choicest among Thy creatures.

These are, O my Lord, the days in which Thou hast bidden Thy servants to observe the fast. Blessed is he that observeth the fast wholly for Thy sake and with absolute detachment from all things except Thee. Assist me and assist them, O my Lord, to obey Thee and to keep Thy precepts. Thou, verily, hast power to do what Thou choosest.

There is no God but Thee, the All-Knowing, the All-Wise. All praise be to God, the Lord of all worlds.   *—Bahá'u'lláh*

23.

THESE ARE, O my God, the days whereon Thou didst enjoin Thy servants to observe the fast. With it Thou didst adorn the preamble of the Book of Thy Laws revealed unto Thy creatures, and didst deck forth the Repositories of Thy commandments in the sight of all who are in Thy heaven and all who are on Thy earth. Thou hast endowed every hour of these days with a special virtue, inscrutable to all except Thee, Whose knowledge embraceth all created things. Thou hast, also, assigned unto every soul a portion of this virtue in accordance with the Tablet of Thy decree and the Scriptures of Thine irrevocable judgment. Every leaf of these Books and Scriptures Thou hast, moreover, allotted to each one of the peoples and kindreds of the earth.

For Thine ardent lovers Thou hast, according to Thy decree, reserved, at each daybreak, the cup of Thy remembrance, O Thou Who art the Ruler of rulers! These are they who have been so inebriated with the wine of Thy manifold wisdom that they forsake their couches in their longing to celebrate Thy praise and extol Thy virtues, and flee from sleep in their eagerness to approach Thy presence and partake of Thy bounty. Their eyes have, at all times, been bent upon the Day-Spring of Thy loving-kindness, and their faces set towards the Fountain-Head of Thine inspiration. Rain down, then, upon us and upon them from the clouds of Thy mercy what beseemeth the heaven of Thy bounteousness and grace.

Lauded be Thy name, O my God! This is the hour when Thou hast unlocked the doors of Thy bounty before the faces of Thy creatures, and opened wide the portals of Thy tender mercy unto all the dwellers of Thine earth. I beseech Thee, by all them whose blood was shed in Thy path, who, in their yearning over Thee, rid themselves from all attachment to any of Thy creatures, and who were so carried away by the sweet savors of Thine inspiration that every single member of their bodies intoned Thy praise and vibrated to Thy remembrance, not to withhold from us the things Thou hast irrevocably ordained in this Revelation—a Revelation the potency of which hath caused every tree to cry out what the Burning Bush had aforetime proclaimed unto Moses, Who conversed with Thee, a Revelation that hath enabled every least pebble to resound again with Thy praise, as the stones glorified Thee in the days of Muḥammad, Thy Friend.

These are the ones, O my God, whom Thou hast graciously enabled to have fellowship with Thee and to commune with Him Who is the Revealer of Thyself. The winds of Thy will have scattered them abroad until Thou didst gather them together beneath Thy shadow, and didst cause them to enter into the precincts of Thy court. Now that Thou hast made them to abide under the shade of the canopy of Thy mercy, do Thou assist them to attain what must befit so august a station. Suffer them not, O my Lord, to be numbered with them who, though enjoying near access to Thee, have been kept back from recognizing Thy face, and who, though meeting with Thee, are deprived of Thy presence.

These are Thy servants, O my Lord, who have entered with Thee in this, the Most Great Prison, who have kept the fast within its walls according to what Thou hadst commanded them in the Tablets of Thy decree and the Books of Thy behest. Send down, therefore, upon them what will thoroughly purge them of all Thou abhorrest, that they may be wholly devoted to Thee, and may detach themselves entirely from all except Thyself.

Rain down, then, upon us, O my God, that which beseemeth Thy grace and befitteth Thy bounty. Enable us, then, O my God, to live in remembrance of Thee and to die in love of Thee, and supply us with the gift of Thy presence in Thy worlds hereafter—worlds which are inscrutable to all except Thee. Thou art our Lord and the Lord of all worlds, and the God of all that are in heaven and all that are on earth.

Thou beholdest, O my God, what hath befallen Thy dear ones in Thy days. Thy glory beareth me witness! The voice of the lamentation of Thy chosen ones hath been lifted up throughout Thy realm. Some were ensnared by the infidels in Thy land, and were hindered by them from having near access to Thee and from attaining the court of Thy glory. Others were able to approach Thee, but were kept back from beholding Thy face. Still others were permitted, in their eagerness to look upon Thee, to enter the precincts of Thy court, but they allowed the veils of the imaginations of Thy creatures and the wrongs inflicted by the oppressors among Thy people to come in between them and Thee.

This is the hour, O my Lord, which Thou hast caused to excel every other hour, and hast related it to the choicest among Thy creatures. I beseech Thee, O my God, by Thy Self and by them, to ordain in the course of this year what shall exalt Thy loved ones. Do Thou, moreover, decree within this year what will enable the Day-Star of Thy power to shine brightly above the horizon of Thy glory, and to illuminate by Thy sovereign might, the whole world.

Render Thy Cause victorious, O my Lord, and abase Thou Thine enemies. Write down, then, for us the good of this life and of the life to come. Thou art the Truth, Who knoweth the secret things. No God is there but Thee, the Ever-Forgiving, the All-Bountiful.

—*Bahá'u'lláh*

24.

GLORY BE to Thee, O Lord my God! These are the days whereon Thou hast bidden all men to observe the fast, that through it they may purify their souls and rid themselves of all attachment to any one but Thee, and that out of their hearts may ascend that which will be worthy of the court of Thy majesty and may well beseem the seat of the revelation of Thy oneness. Grant, O my Lord, that this fast may become a river of life-giving waters, and may yield the virtue wherewith Thou hast endowed it. Cleanse Thou by its means the hearts of Thy servants whom the evils of the world have failed to hinder from turning towards Thine all-glorious Name, and who have remained unmoved by the noise and tumult of such as have repudiated Thy most resplendent signs which have accompanied the advent of Thy Manifestation Whom Thou hast invested with Thy sovereignty, Thy power, Thy majesty and glory. These are the servants who, as soon as Thy call reached them, hastened in the direction of Thy mercy and were not kept back from Thee by the changes and chances of this world or by any human limitations.

I am he, O my God, who testifieth to Thy unity, who acknowledgeth Thy oneness, who boweth humbly before the revelations of Thy majesty, and who recognizeth with downcast countenance the splendors of the light of Thy transcendent glory. I have believed in Thee after Thou didst enable me to know Thy Self, Whom Thou hast revealed to men's eyes through the power of Thy sovereignty and might. Unto Him I have turned, wholly detached from all things, and cleaving steadfastly unto the cord of Thy gifts and favors. I have embraced His truth, and the truth of all the wondrous laws and precepts that have been sent down unto Him. I have fasted for love of Thee and in pursuance of Thine injunction, and have broken my fast with Thy praise on my tongue and in conformity with Thy pleasure. Suffer me not, O my Lord, to be reckoned among them who have fasted in the daytime, who in the night-season have prostrated themselves before Thy face, and who have repudiated Thy truth, disbelieved in Thy signs, gainsaid Thy testimony, and perverted Thine utterances.

Open Thou, O my Lord, mine eyes and the eyes of all them that have sought Thee, that we may recognize Thee with Thine own eyes. This is Thy bidding given us in the Book sent down by Thee unto Him Whom Thou hast chosen by Thy behest, Whom Thou hast singled out for Thy favor above all Thy creatures, Whom Thou hast been pleased to invest with Thy sovereignty, and Whom Thou hast specially favored and entrusted with Thy Message unto Thy people. Praised be Thou, therefore, O my God, inasmuch as Thou hast graciously enabled us to recognize Him and to acknowledge whatsoever hath been sent down unto Him, and conferred upon us the honor of attaining the presence of the One Whom Thou didst promise in Thy Book and in Thy Tablets.

Thou seest me then, O my God, with my face turned toward Thee, cleaving steadfastly to the cord of Thy gracious providence and generosity, and clinging to the hem of Thy tender mercies and bountiful favors. Destroy not, I implore Thee, my hopes of attaining unto that which Thou didst ordain for Thy servants who have turned towards the precincts of Thy court and the sanctuary of Thy presence, and have observed the fast for love of Thee. I confess, O my God, that whatever proceedeth from me is wholly unworthy of Thy sovereignty and falleth short of Thy majesty. And yet I beseech Thee by Thy Name through which Thou hast revealed Thy Self, in the glory of Thy most excellent titles, unto all created things, in this Revelation whereby Thou hast, through Thy most resplendent Name, manifested Thy beauty, to give me to drink of the wine of Thy mercy and of the pure beverage of Thy favor, which have streamed forth from the right hand of Thy will, that I may so fix my gaze upon Thee and be so detached from all else but Thee, that the world and all that hath been created therein may appear before me as a fleeting day which Thou hast not deigned to create.

I moreover entreat Thee, O my God, to rain down, from the heaven of Thy will and the clouds of Thy mercy, that which will cleanse us from the noisome savors of our transgressions, O Thou Who hast called Thyself the God of

Mercy! Thou art, verily, the Most Powerful, the All-Glorious, the Beneficent.

Cast not away, O my Lord, him that hath turned toward Thee, nor suffer him who hath drawn nigh unto Thee to be removed far from Thy court. Dash not the hopes of the suppliant who hath longingly stretched out his hands to seek Thy grace and favors, and deprive not Thy sincere servants of the wonders of Thy tender mercies and loving-kindness. Forgiving and Most Bountiful art Thou, O my Lord! Power hast Thou to do what Thou pleasest. All else but Thee are impotent before the revelations of Thy might, are as lost in the face of the evidences of Thy wealth, are as nothing when compared with the manifestations of Thy transcendent sovereignty, and are destitute of all strength when face to face with the signs and tokens of Thy power. What refuge is there beside Thee, O my Lord, to which I can flee, and where is there a haven to which I can hasten? Nay, the power of Thy might beareth me witness! No protector is there but Thee; no place to flee to except Thee, no refuge to seek save Thee. Cause me to taste, O my Lord, the divine sweetness of Thy remembrance and praise. I swear by Thy might! Whosoever tasteth of its sweetness will rid himself of all attachment to the world and all that is therein, and will set his face toward Thee, cleansed from the remembrance of any one except Thee.

Inspire then my soul, O my God, with Thy wondrous remembrance, that I may glorify Thy name. Number me not with them who read Thy words and fail to find Thy hidden gift which, as decreed by Thee, is contained therein, and which quickeneth the souls of Thy creatures and the hearts of Thy servants. Cause me, O my Lord, to be reckoned among them who have been so stirred up by the sweet savors that have been wafted in Thy days that they have laid down their lives for Thee and hastened to the scene of their death in their longing to gaze on Thy beauty and in their yearning to attain Thy presence. And were any one to say unto them on their way, "Whither go ye?" they would say, "Unto God, the All-Possessing, the Help in Peril, the Self-Subsisting!"

The transgressions committed by such as have turned away from Thee and have borne themselves haughtily toward Thee have not availed to hinder them from loving Thee, and from setting their faces toward Thee, and from turning in the direction of Thy mercy. These are they who are blessed by the Concourse on high, who are glorified by the denizens of the everlasting Cities, and beyond them by those on whose foreheads Thy most exalted pen hath written: "These! The people of Bahá. Through them have been shed the splendors of the light of guidance." Thus hath it been ordained, at Thy behest and by Thy will, in the Tablet of Thine irrevocable decree.

Proclaim, therefore, O my God, their greatness and the greatness of those who while living or after death have circled round them. Supply them with that which Thou hast ordained for the righteous among Thy creatures. Potent art Thou to do all things. There is no God but Thee, the All-Powerful, the Help in Peril, the Almighty, the Most Bountiful.

Do not bring our fasts to an end with this fast, O my Lord, nor the covenants Thou hast made with this covenant. Do Thou accept all that we have done for love of Thee, and for the sake of Thy pleasure, and all that we have left undone as a result of our subjection to our evil and corrupt desires. Enable us, then, to cleave steadfastly to Thy love and Thy good-pleasure, and preserve us from the mischief of such as have denied Thee and repudiated Thy most resplendent signs. Thou art, in truth, the Lord of this world and of the next. No God is there beside Thee, the Exalted, the Most High.

Magnify Thou, O Lord my God, Him Who is the Primal Point, the Divine Mystery, the Unseen Essence, the Day-Spring of Divinity, and the Manifestation of Thy Lordship, through Whom all the knowledge of the past and all the knowledge of the future were made plain, through Whom the pearls of Thy hidden wisdom were uncovered, and the mystery of Thy treasured name disclosed, Whom Thou hast appointed as the Announcer of the One through Whose name the letter B and the letter E have been joined and united, through Whom Thy majesty, Thy sovereignty and Thy might were made known, through Whom Thy words have been sent down, and Thy laws set forth with clearness, and Thy signs spread abroad, and Thy Word established, through Whom the hearts of Thy chosen ones were laid bare, and all that were in the heavens and all that were on the earth were gathered together, whom Thou hast called 'Alí-Muhammad in the kingdom of Thy names, and the Spirit of Spirits in the Tablets of Thine irrevocable decree, Whom Thou hast invested with Thine own title, unto Whose name all other names have, at Thy bidding and through the power of Thy might, been made to return, and in Whom Thou hast caused all Thine attributes and titles to attain their final consummation. To Him also belong such names as lay hid within Thy stainless tabernacles, in Thine invisible world and Thy sanctified cities.

Magnify Thou, moreover, such as have believed in Him and in His signs and have turned toward Him, from among those that have acknowledged Thy unity in His Latter Manifestation—a Manifestation whereof He hath made mention in His Tablets, and in His Books, and in His Scriptures, and in all the wondrous verses and gem-like utterances that have descended upon Him. It is this same Manifestation Whose Covenant Thou hast bidden Him establish ere He had established His own Covenant. He it is Whose praise the Bayán hath celebrated. In it His excellence hath been extolled, and His truth established, and His sovereignty proclaimed, and His Cause perfected. Blessed is the man that hath turned unto Him, and fulfilled the things He hath commanded, O Thou Who art the Lord of the worlds and the Desire of all them that have known Thee!

Praised be Thou, O my God, inasmuch as

Thou hast aided us to recognize and love Him. I, therefore, beseech Thee by Him and by them Who are the Day-Springs of Thy Divinity, and the Manifestations of Thy Lordship, and the Treasuries of Thy Revelation, and the Depositories of Thine inspiration, to enable us to serve and obey Him, and to empower us to become the helpers of His Cause and the dispersers of His adversaries. Powerful art Thou to do all that pleaseth Thee. No God is there beside Thee, the Almighty, the All-Glorious, the One Whose help is sought by all men!

—*Bahá'u'lláh*

Naw-Rúz

25.

(Naw-Rúz, March 21, is the first day of the Bahá'í year.)

PRAISED be Thou, O my God, that Thou hast ordained Naw-Rúz as a festival unto those who have observed the fast for love of Thee and abstained from all that is abhorrent unto Thee. Grant, O my Lord, that the fire of Thy love and the heat produced by the fast enjoined by Thee may inflame them in Thy Cause, and make them to be occupied with Thy praise and with remembrance of Thee.

Since Thou hast adorned them, O my Lord, with the ornament of the fast prescribed by Thee, do Thou adorn them also with the ornament of Thine acceptance, through Thy grace and bountiful favor. For the doings of men are all dependent upon Thy good-pleasure, and are conditioned by Thy behest. Shouldst Thou regard him who hath broken the fast as one who hath observed it, such a man would be reckoned among them who from eternity had been keeping the fast. And shouldst Thou decree that he who hath observed the fast hath broken it, that person would be numbered with such as have caused the Robe of Thy Revelation to be stained with dust, and been far removed from the crystal waters of this living Fountain.

Thou art He through Whom the ensign "Praiseworthy art Thou in Thy works" hath been lifted up, and the standard "Obeyed art Thou in Thy behest" hath been unfurled. Make known this Thy station, O my God, unto Thy servants, that they may be made aware that the excellence of all things is dependent upon Thy bidding and Thy word, and the virtue of every act is conditioned by Thy leave and the good-pleasure of Thy will, and may recognize that the reins of men's doings are within the grasp of Thine acceptance and Thy commandment. Make this known unto them, that nothing whatsoever may shut them out from Thy Beauty, in these days whereon the Christ exclaimeth: "All dominion is Thine, O Thou the Begetter of the Spirit (Jesus)"; and Thy Friend (Muḥammad) crieth out: "Glory be to Thee, O Thou the Best-Beloved, for that Thou hast uncovered Thy

Beauty, and written down for Thy chosen ones what will cause them to attain unto the seat of the revelation of Thy Most Great Name, through which all the peoples have lamented except such as have detached themselves from all else except Thee, and set themselves towards Him Who is the Revealer of Thyself and the Manifestation of Thine attributes."

He Who is Thy Branch and all Thy company, O my Lord, have broken this day their fast, after having observed it within the precincts of Thy court, and in their eagerness to please Thee. Do Thou ordain for him, and for them, and for all such as have entered Thy presence in those days all the good Thou didst destine in Thy Book. Supply them, then, with that which will profit them, in both this life and in the life beyond.

Thou, in truth, art the All-Knowing, the All-Wise. —*Bahá'u'lláh*

Marriage

"But the Bahá'í engagement is the perfect communication and the entire consent of both parties. However, they must show forth the utmost attention and become informed of one another's character and the firm covenant made between each other must become an eternal binding, and their intentions must be everlasting affinity, friendship, unity and life."—'Abdu'l-Bahá.

The pledge of marriage, the phrase to be spoken individually by the bride and the bridegroom in the presence of Bahá'í witnesses, as stipulated in the *Kitáb-i-Aqdas* (The Most Holy Book), is: *"We will all, verily, abide by the Will of God."*

26.

HE IS the Generous, the All-Bountiful!

Praise be to God, the Ancient, the Ever-Abiding, the Changeless, the Eternal! He Who hath testified in His Own Being that verily He is the One, the Single, the Untrammelled, the Exalted. We bear witness that verily there is no God but Him; acknowledging His oneness, confessing His singleness. He hath ever dwelt in unapproachable heights, in the summits of His loftiness, sanctified from the mention of aught save Himself, free from the description of aught but Him.

And when He desired to manifest grace and beneficence to men, and to set the world in order, He revealed observances and created laws; among them He established the law of marriage, made it as a fortress for well-being and salvation, and enjoined it upon us in that which was sent down out of the heaven of sanctity in His Most Holy Book. He saith, great is His glory: "Marry, O people, that from you may appear he who will remember Me amongst My servants; this is one of My commandments unto you; obey it as an assistance to yourselves."

—Bahá'u'lláh

27.

HE IS God! O peerless Lord! In Thine almighty wisdom Thou hast enjoined marriage upon the peoples, that the generations of men may succeed one another in this contingent world, and that ever, so long as the world shall last, they may busy themselves at the threshold of Thy oneness with servitude and worship, with salutation, adoration and praise. "I have not created spirits and men, but that they should worship me." [1] Wherefore, wed Thou in the heaven of Thy mercy these two birds of the nest of Thy love, and make them the means of attracting perpetual grace; that from the union of these two seas of love a wave of tenderness may surge and cast the pearls of pure and goodly issue on the shore of life. "He hath let loose the two seas, that they meet each other: Between them is a barrier which they overpass not. Which then of the bounties of your Lord will ye deny? From each He bringeth up greater and lesser pearls." [2]

O Thou kind Lord! Make Thou this marriage to bring forth coral and pearls. Thou art verily the All-Powerful, the Most Great, the Ever-Forgiving!   —'Abdu'l-Bahá

28.

GLORY BE unto Thee, O my God! Verily, this Thy servant and this Thy maid-servant have gathered under the shadow of Thy mercy and

[1] Qur'án, 51:56.
[2] Qur'án, 55:19-22.